Bike Ride
with a
Twist

8,321 kilometres
across Canada

Janice Kenyon

to Pat –
Happy pedalling !
Janice K.

Kachina Press

Photos by Janice Kenyon. Climbing, Québec City and Sailing the St. Lawrence Seaway by John Ngai.
Author photo by George Heffelfinger.
Edited by Shawn England
Maps by Nader Salloum, Digital Projections, www.digitalpro.ca
Design by Andrea Belcher
Printed and bound in Canada by Friesens Corporation

Published by
Kachina Press
609 Riverside Blvd. NW
High River, AB T1V 2C1

Copies available from Kachina Press and www.bikecanadawithatwist.com.

Library and Archives Canada Cataloguing in Publication

Kenyon, Janice, 1938-

Bike ride with a twist: 8,321 km across Canada / Janice Kenyon.

Includes bibliographical references.
ISBN 0-9692194-4-X

1. Cycling – Canada. 2. Canada – Description and travel.
3. Kenyon, Janice, 1938 – Travel – Canada. 1. Title.

FC75.K45 2006   917.0472

C2006-900950-3

For all cyclists who have pedalled across the whole or parts of Canada, or who dream of making the journey someday. Canada makes dreams come true – go for it!

Cross-Canada Bike Route

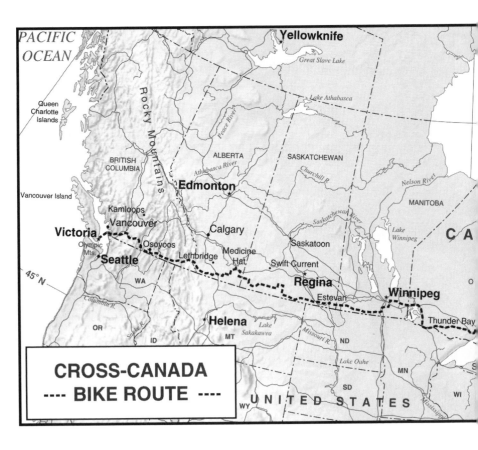

CROSS-CANADA
---- BIKE ROUTE ----

Acknowledgments

Neither my ride nor this book would have happened without the support of friends, family, and all the strangers – both Canadians and non-Canadians – who gave encouragement and assistance along the way. I cannot thank each of you enough!

Valuable editing from Shawn England, plus numerous hours of diligent digital mapping from Nader Salloum of Digital Projections in Calgary kept the book alive and well through months of design and formatting from Andrea Belcher. I am grateful to each of you.

Special mention to Ross, Art, Dirk, Sharon, and Monique for sharing their partners' dreams while they were left behind. Go, grandma, go! echoes all the grandchildren's cheers that will no doubt outlive both me and this book. Lance Armstrong and Jack Layton have been inspirations to keep pedalling. There's always one more hill, and sometimes the wind is at our backs.

Contents

Contents cont'd

Introduction

There's no doubt about it. My bike ride across the United States in the spring of 2003 was the impetus for my 2004 cross-Canada odyssey. It was in the U.S. where I experienced camping while biking, all the while conquering demons of doubt in my head. With time, I found that I could do it. Riding long distances with my whole world strapped to my bike became second nature; my first instinct became saving myself from threats along the route, both human and natural.

Across the southern U.S. there were sandstorms, tumbleweeds, dogs and deer and poisonous snakes. There were kamikaze truck drivers who were equally as threatening as the crazies in my group. Human dynamics vied for attention with flat tires, pot holes, and roadkill. The negatives threatened to drown the positives, but natural beauty was persistent. Gullies of wildflowers collided in kaleidoscopes of colour. There were cooling dips in rivers with cypress trees rising from flowing currents. Hot sun drilling through granite canyons gave warmth in the chilly mountains. Star-strewn galaxies emerged at midnight when the wind dropped, my tent stopped vibrating, and I returned from the Land of Oz. Careening down the Yellow Brick Road wrapped in my flimsy nylon bedroom had seemed an imminent possibility.

Would any of this have happened any other way than on my bike, under any other conditions? Decidedly not.

It was two months before my sixty-fifth birthday when I pedalled across the U.S., a long-retired registered nurse, unemployed except for writing non-fiction books that have appeared every few years. After emigrating to Canada from the U.S. in 1973, I settled on Vancouver Island with my British-born husband. Retirement brought a move to Scotland for a few years before returning to Canada and the foothills of the Rockies in 2001. Early explorations of Canada's west-coast islands and then Scotland and more of Europe by bike have continuously pushed my boundaries, but long-distance touring and camping had been a dream I did not expect to become reality.

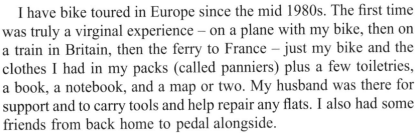

I have bike toured in Europe since the mid 1980s. The first time was truly a virginal experience – on a plane with my bike, then on a train in Britain, then the ferry to France – just my bike and the clothes I had in my packs (called panniers) plus a few toiletries, a book, a notebook, and a map or two. My husband was there for support and to carry tools and help repair any flats. I also had some friends from back home to pedal alongside.

I went back several times. France, Germany, Austria, Scandinavia, Italy, Greece, Britain. In Norway there were longer distances, higher bridges, very scary tunnels – all exciting challenges! In 2002, while researching Cuba by bike on the Internet for a two-week sprint there, my computer discovered a tour across the southern U.S. that sounded feasible, if I was allowed to join the group at my age. More research, phone calls, emails, and recommendations told me I could do it, and I would not be the oldest in the group (the other was older by only a few months, it turned out). I signed on for April and May of 2003. My husband wasn't interested in camping or cycling the long distances, but I could live my dream with a group for social support as well as mechanical backup, all the while being self-sufficient in a tent.

Just how self-sufficient I had yet to discover. At first I was surprised by my isolation within the group; it felt like no one was there to help or share or ride with. But after a few shared flat-tire repairs, along with shared cooking for the group after pedalling endless hours of rural, lonely roads, with perhaps one or two others, we got to know each other better. By the end, we had travelled together for sixty-one days and covered 5,160 kilometres. I now realize we were all pedalling down the same road – isolated, vulnerable, scared of all the unknowns and dangers. Gradually we adapted – to each other and the ride, and in the end some of us became friends. And we certainly learned a lot – about camping, being self-sufficient, group interactions, and riding our bikes for many hours while seemingly going nowhere. But we were going somewhere.

Eventually we got there. From the Pacific to the Atlantic. We smelled the flowers, dodged roadkill including poisonous snakes, watched the sun creep over or descend into the horizon, sweated in the deserts, shivered in the mountains, sang nonsense verses to break the boredom on lonely stretches, cried when one of us got hit by a car (but was not seriously injured), then drank ourselves silly at our farewell dinner – none of which would have happened if we hadn't been on our bikes. Did we feel special, unique, privileged, content on our last day? Decidedly, yes!

And Canada beckoned! All 8,321 kilometres over 105 days in the summer of 2004. It wasn't long after the U.S. ride before I knew I would do Canada. I could go the distance, I could take care of myself, and I had come to grips with being alone and learning that I would never be totally alone for long; someone somewhere would offer help if and when I needed it. And that's a big item – having confidence in yourself and your world, as unusual and isolated as it may be, while allaying crippling fears that can spoil a beautiful bike ride.

I didn't aspire to travelling down the world's longest river in a two-man raft, or climbing the earth's highest mountain without oxygen, or skiing solo across the South Pole. I just wanted to ride my bike across Canada, but preliminary research quickly showed me that this would be a bike ride with a twist if I wanted to stay completely north of the Canada/U.S. border while using roads less travelled than the TransCanada Highway.

Most trans-Canada cyclists dip into the U.S. to avoid the long distances around Lake of the Woods and Lake Superior. But the wildness and isolation of these areas hold a special fascination for me, and I didn't want to miss them. They are part of the wilderness that makes Canada unique, and I certainly wanted to give these areas a try.

Avoiding the TransCanada Highway was the other big challenge in planning the route. I could follow the highway along with the trucks and do the whole thing in about ten weeks, if I didn't mind the traffic and the fumes and the dangerous conditions. But I did mind, so I planned a route using lesser roads and taking more time – a total of fourteen weeks plus one extra for good measure.

I advertised for company at local bike shops in my hometown of Canmore, Alberta. I also alerted my fellow Canadian on the U.S. ride who is a retired lawyer/educator/business administrator from Montreal. Other friends expressed interest in going part way. By the time May 1st arrived there were three of us aspiring to go all the way: myself, Marg, a retired cashier who quickly transformed into

Granny M while realizing her dream of cycling across Canada, and Jean Joseph, the retired lawyer/educator/business administrator from Montreal, who naturally settled into being our Grand Père on the ride. By mid-April he emailed that he had bought a plane ticket for Vancouver and would meet us in Victoria, B.C. with his bike on the appointed day. Two others would come part way in the west, and two others hoped to meet us in Québec for part of the east.

So we were a motley crowd on Departure Day, six of us on bikes, all wanting to see Canada (or parts of it) from its English west to its French east, while we established a southern bike route across one of the widest countries in the world using back roads and bike trails. We would scoop the mountains, beat the grasshoppers, zigzag across the Shield, wave at Winnie the Pooh, *parler français*, maybe shake hands with Anne at Green Gables, and finally camp beside ponds in Newfoundland. We would pedal exclusively in Canada. We would be happy, sad, frustrated, scared, relieved, grateful, tired, and sore. And we would be elated when we got to St. John's, Newfoundland. Will the city ever know how important it was in our scheme of adventuring? Probably not. Will there be an end to our adventures? I doubt it. But at ages fifty-seven to sixty-six (in 2004), how many more twists can we discover?

How to Use This Book

Highlights

Highlights are a travelogue based on my encounters with the history, culture, and landscape of each province. The episodes described are not necessarily in chronological order.

Logistics

Logistics are in chronological order following my route in consecutive days of travel. After British Columbia, camping is the norm on the trip. When not camping, campgrounds are listed as alternatives to motels. After British Columbia, motels used as diversion from inclement weather are indicated by parentheses in **Ride**.

Ride: Destination of each day's ride followed by route; terrain of route; tourist diversions if unusual or significant for area. Helpful hints for isolated areas, i.e., "carry lots of water."

Facilities: Services available along route. Overnight services, both motels and camping. Bike shops that I used en route (there are more in major centres).

Total distance: what I clocked on my personal cyclometre (which may vary with actual distances on map; also, I have used distances clocked by other cyclists on routes I did not cycle).

Average speed: included wherever I recorded it in my notes (some days are missing along with all of B.C. for which I apologize). Average speed is a helpful guide to the difficulty of the ride. As my average speed on my old, heavy Trek 520 steel bike was fairly high (most tourers consider fourteen kilometres per hour a good average speed) and I do not consider myself a fast rider (compared to others), my average is probably a reasonable indicator of touring across Canada while riding fully loaded. I carried approximately twelve kilograms (twenty-six pounds) of gear. As an example: my average speed in Newfoundland varied

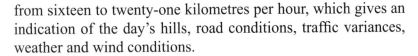

from sixteen to twenty-one kilometres per hour, which gives an indication of the day's hills, road conditions, traffic variances, weather and wind conditions.

A note on wind and weather: wind can slow cycling speed considerably, especially on flat terrain. Consult maps and route along with average speed for degrees of difficulty.

Maximum speed: given as another indication of degrees of hills. High maximum only happens on steep downhills with minimal headwind! As an example: On day 104, I record an average speed of sixteen kilometres per hour with a maximum speed of sixty kilometres per hour over a total distance of 103 kilometres – all indicators of high hills that take a long time to summit, and not a lot of wind to slow on downhills.

A Note on Trip Planning

Obtain the toll-free telephone numbers of each province's Tourism Department from your local provincial Tourist Information Centre. Inform each province of your plans and ask for any information they may have regarding cycling in their province plus their current tourism booklets. They will send you (free of charge) their accommodation and camping guides, as well as their official highway road maps. The only province that did not send me their guides and highway map was Saskatchewan despite repeated phone requests from me. Eventually I purchased a Saskatchewan road map which was easily obtained as I live in an adjacent province. Then I consulted with friends who knew the area to plan my route (which turned out to be more isolated than proposed, but also more adventurous and certainly a route less-travelled than other busier roads). There is also information on each province's web site.

Maps

Official highway maps from each province are basic planning tools. Do not use the abbreviated versions published by automobile associations.

Trans Canada Trail maps are on www.tctrail.ca and available in book form for various areas. I used Mussio Ventures & Trails BC Present *Trans Canada Trail the British Columbia Route*, available from Mussio Ventures, 232 Anthony Court, New Westminster, B.C. V3L 5T5, www.backroadmapbooks.com.

Kettle Valley Railway maps are available in the book *Cycling the Kettle Valley Railway* by Dan & Sandra Langford published by Rocky Mountain Books, #4 Spruce Centre SW, Calgary, AB T3C 3B3, www.rmbooks.com.

La Route Verte, the Green Route, publishes a coil-bound book of their entire bike route system for Québec. *Take a Ride on the Green Side* is available from Vélo Québec, 1251 Rue Rachel Est, Montréal, Québec H2J 2J9, www.routeverte.com. The province of Québec sent me several La Route Verte brochures containing abbreviated maps (including Le Petit Temis) along with their tourist information.

Regional bike route maps are available from local Tourist Information Centres, sometimes with surprising revelations. Many areas have off-road trails suitable for all types of bikes and bypassing major roads. For example, I obtained a map for cycling the Oliver Area in B.C. that took me off a busy highway in the Okanagan Valley; Galloping Goose trail maps are available at several outlets in Victoria, B.C.; the Ottawa River Parkway is on most Ottawa city maps as well as individual bike route maps available from tourist centres in the area.

My regional research for the Bruce Peninsula area of Ontario told me there was a bike trail along the southern shore of Georgian Bay that avoided heavy road traffic. When I arrived in the area I couldn't find an area map and asked local cyclists for directions to the trail access. When researching this area, I had spoken with other cyclists who didn't know about this trail and complained about the heavy traffic (one cycling friend suffered serious injuries when hit by a car near Wasaga Beach). This would have been a deterrent to using my route through eastern Ontario; knowing about the trail encouraged me to follow my plan to avoid the unsafe TransCanada Highway north of Georgian Bay.

I mapped my entire route before leaving home, which was definitely a tentative plan but surprisingly accurate in terms of both time and route. Friends and family back home could follow my progress, and I was reassured that all my hours of research and planning was productive. Planning takes time; allow at least several months to learn about your route before beginning your ride. Some cyclists spend years planning a trip of this magnitude; some take off on a whim, I know, but perhaps they miss a lot of what Canada has to offer to the touring cyclist.

Abbreviations

KVR: Kettle Valley Railway
T.C.H.: TransCanada Highway
PEI: Prince Edward Island
km: kilometres
kph: kilometres per hour
T. I.: Tourist Information
TCT: Trans Canada Trail

Metric Conversions

1 km = 0.6 mile
   100 km = 60 miles, 20 kph = 12 miles per hour
10 metres = 32 feet
   100 m = 328 feet
10 centimetres = almost 4 inches
   2.5 cm = 1 inch
30 degrees Celsius = 86 degrees Fahrenheit

Glossary

braze-on: brazing or joining two pieces of tubing when bicycle is manufactured using specific material with specific melting points – very difficult to replicate after frame has been built.

cyclometre: battery operated cycle computer that clips onto handlebars and measures total distance, current ride distance, current and average and maximum speed, total time pedalling, twenty-four-hour clock time. Some computers have added features including heart rate monitors. Most cyclometres can be set for either miles or kilometres.

derailleurs: transmission mechanisms that change gears (guides the chain up or down); separate mechanisms for front chain rings and rear cogsets.

headset: connects the fork (holds and turns the front wheel) through the head tube to the handlebars to allow the bike to be steered.

pannier: pack that clips onto front or rear bike rack

psi or pounds per square inch: measurement of air pressure in tires

sag car or wagon: vehicle accompaniment on bike tour. Usually carries equipment, supplies, tools, and sometimes offers space for injured or tired cyclists; on large group tours often carries extra bikes as well as bike parts

British Columbia

License plate motto: Beautiful British Columbia
Official flower: Pacific dogwood
Official bird: Steller's jay

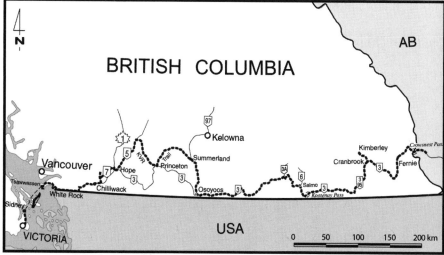

Route across British Columbia

Going down the highway
Going nowhere
Seeking some adventure
To feed my soul
~ Janice Kenyon

Highlights

May 1, 2004. Mile Zero, Victoria, B.C., Vancouver Island, Canada. A stone and wooden monument marks the spot: 4,879 miles of the TransCanada Highway ends – or begins – here, then crosses ten provinces to link Canada from coast to coast. The highway was completed and paved end-to-end in 1970, before Canada went metric, so the marker indicates miles instead of kilometres. But we know it will be close to 8,000 kilometre clicks on our cyclometres by the time we are all the way across.

We are six cyclists gathered under sunny skies at Mile Zero to begin our own coast to coast trek. For two of us it is more the idea than the doing: Irene, my dear friend and cycling buddy who lives in Victoria, is able to pedal only as far as the ferry; Paul, another Victoria native, pedalled in France with me a few years ago, and is joining the group only for the first week. Lynda, a friend from up-island who has taken up triathlon racing, will cover the first province; Granny M, Grand Père and myself are hitching our hopes on covering all ten. We are four females and two males, all grandparents. Five of us are western Canadians (Irene and Paul are bilingual), and Grand Père brings a welcome French Canadian accent to our adventure.

Several boisterous grandchildren join the fray at our send-off. They help to ease the emotion, waving and playing, oblivious to the larger significance of the occasion. Cameras click non-stop. Finally, we grandmas and grandpas, on our assortment of two wheelers with panniers and other bike packs, make our way through downtown Victoria onto the Galloping Goose, an historic abandoned rail bed that takes us forty-five kilometres all the way to the ferry. What a treat! A propitious beginning on the Trans Canada Trail system. No car traffic – just cyclists and hikers – and a picturesque ride quieter than the original "gawky and noisy gas rail-car" that the trail is named after – quieter until we all compete for conversation, some of which is nervous chatter. This is Day One, plus it is our shakedown ride. We haven't tested either our equipment or ourselves as a group before today.

Four-and-a-half hours from Mile Zero we are waiting for the ferry to the mainland. We found a spot to dip our rear wheels in the Pacific Ocean before leaving Victoria, then we bid Irene a sad farewell (she really wanted to come all the way) at the ferry terminal before stashing our bikes at the front of the ferry's car deck. So far so good. No last minute trips to the bike shop. No major adjustments. A little less chatter now.

Once off the ferry we turn into the port town of Tsawwassen and a small motel. Everyone is beginning to relax. Paul, the golfer amongst us, heads for the private golf club across the street. Can he talk them into serving us dinner? Yes! It's a great evening: nice food, a glass or two of wine. A good omen, I tell myself. The only person who knew everyone before was me, so there's a lot of getting-acquainted to do. We even manage a group laundry – all our sweaty bike clothes into one load. Then it doesn't take us long to hit the pillow. Only fifty-two kilometres on the cyclometer, but the departure has been intense for each of us. Grand Père and I have done cross-continent tours carrying our own gear; Paul has done some independent European touring (with my husband and myself);

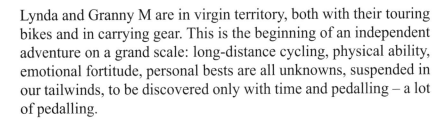

Lynda and Granny M are in virgin territory, both with their touring bikes and in carrying gear. This is the beginning of an independent adventure on a grand scale: long-distance cycling, physical ability, emotional fortitude, personal bests are all unknowns, suspended in our tailwinds, to be discovered only with time and pedalling – a lot of pedalling.

The next morning we head north, then east, then south, from Tsawwassen to the Canada/U.S. border. Unlike the U.S./Mexico border on the opposite edge of the United States, there are no border patrols or fences. Just obelisk markers along the forty-ninth parallel, in a ditch one can cross in one step. But no one does. This is a cross-Canada bike ride!

We follow "0 Avenue" that runs parallel to the forty-ninth parallel, and eventually end in Abbotsford at our pre-booked motel. It's twenty degrees Celsius at 2:00 in the afternoon and my cyclometre reads eighty-one kilometres for the day. If we weren't in shape before, it's going to happen quickly! A swim and hot tub at the motel pool ease aching muscles and tender bums.

The next day is another long ride to Harrison Hot Springs, but again we catch part of the Trans Canada Trail, this time along the Sumas River and Vedder Canal between Abbotsford and Chilliwack, and avoid a lot of traffic plus the hills on the north side of the Fraser River. I had previously scouted out the trail leaving Abbotsford following Lynda's suggestions. She used to live in the area, and knew some of the territory.

This whole part of the route has been a real find. I pieced it together with info from other cyclists, plus maps, and the results are amazing. We've been on the ride three days and covered approximately fifteen kilometres on a busy highway out of a total of 210 kilometres, the remaining distance being located on trails or quiet roads. We avoided Vancouver completely, along with the hilly terrain along the Fraser. I can only hope this good luck with the route will continue. From now on it's essentially wait and see.

We'd been told there's a good bike shop in Chilliwack, so we make a quick stop there for some bar-end additions to the one hybrid mountain bike in the group. Already Lynda has some ulnar

Agassiz mural

nerve neuropathy – numbness in her wrists and hands – from the straight handle bars. This was not happening on her shorter training rides. She is just doing British Columbia, but that in itself means a lot of challenging mountain climbs ahead. Hopefully she has found a cure. I check my tire pressures and they are holding at 110 pounds per square inch (psi) – too high, I learn later, the hard way.

During my research for the trip, I was repeatedly confronted with features about murals, often in small, unknown towns that have raised their profiles by having artists paint scenes on their town buildings that relate local history. Some of these otherwise obscure towns have become quite famous because of their murals. At Agassiz I photograph the start of what I hope will become a significant recording of my travels. This one features a large-as-life farm scene: red truck, dairy cows, big barn against a mountain backdrop. We have pedalled past many kilometres of raspberry canes, dairy farms, and other mixed farming being planted – all in the luscious Fraser Valley. There have also been numerous large churches. This is Mennonite country, and we see evidence of prosperity in the large homes and gardens we leave behind.

By lunch time it's drizzling rain – typical west coast weather. The next morning it's still raining lightly; then stretches of inter-mittent drizzle fading to clear off and on. We pedal towards the

Coast Mountains poking through mist or swirls of rising fog – a more appropriate west coast scene could not have been made to order. No one is seriously cold or wet when we reach the mighty Fraser River near Hope early and earn a half-day off. This gives us time for emails and a makeshift repair of the clamp holding a rear rack in place on Granny M's bike. The old clamp (in place after the frame's braze-on for the rack snapped off on a fall from the bike before leaving home) has slipped down onto the chain. This could become an aggravating and chronic mechanical problem. We can only hope that the new clamp holds – a good omen from Hope?

A rain forest introduces us to the famous Kettle Valley Railway (KVR). We follow Kawkawa Lake Road onto a trail scattered with fresh bear scat, but tree roots tangled under over-hanging crags dripping with mist and moss keep us focused on the path. After about ten kilometres, we come face to face with Coquihalla Canyon and four short tunnels that were carved through the granite in the early part of the twentieth century. Railway engineers lowered themselves down the canyon walls in woven baskets to survey the route – and in the 1980s *Rambo* followed suit (without the baskets) for his heroic antics in Sylvester Stallone's action movies filmed in the canyon. I can picture Rambo hanging off the bridges that connect the tunnels, daring the thundering water below to spoil his escape route. The macho superman still rides on his laurels, from what I hear – I wonder what he would think of us cyclists intruding on his set. We pedal out of the canyon, not quite Rambo style, but close.

The railway bed is not ridable after the tunnels, so we move onto the wide shoulder of the Coquihalla Highway. It's a long lung-and-leg-expanding pull to Coquihalla Summit at 1,244 metres in melting snow, a cold tailwind, and rain showers; then an ice-cube descent in spite of spitting sunshine that is unable to keep us warm on the downhill. After another short and steep climb helps us to warm up, at last we descend at Exit 250 as instructed in the KVR guide book, but where is the trail? After searching and descending some more, we stumble on a miniscule Trans Canada Trail sign pointing towards Brookmere at a log bridge crossing a river. Brookmere is our destination and we hope we are on the KVR. Recent logging

Rambo country — Othello tunnels

has made a mess of the trail, and I manage to bend my front fender, accordion style, when a piece of tree catches between my fender and tire. I remove the jagged log and the now-shredded strips of aluminum fender drop back into position where they stay, thank goodness. Duct tape will come in handy here. Fresh bear scat is hardly noticed, but I know this is springtime for the bears. We are all out here exploring and looking for food.

We have a booking at a back-country lodge at Brookmere, which appears after the three of us with road tires (not mountain bike fatties) are reduced to walking our bikes six kilometres over large lumpy rocks and rail-bed ballast on the unmaintained trail. The surface is tough even for mountain bikes, but the two with fatter tires manage to ride some of it. The lodge caters to cyclists and hikers, and the proprietors have supplied groceries for us to fix our own dinner and breakfast plus lunch the next day. The cooking is easy – the lady doing the grocery shopping according to the list I supplied has donated her own wild salmon for grilling – and we manage to get through the evening with this much appreciated treat washed down with a six-pack of beer plus a few bottles of wine. We have climbed our first mountain pass (in some snow), pushed through rain forest and tunnels, and are on the KVR, our route for the next few days – and after ninety-one kilometres, we are all exhausted. We don't even hear each other's snoring in the dormitory-style sleeping area.

Over the next two days we try the KVR again – and again. It is a no-go for skinny tires on loaded touring bikes. So we are out on the secondary roads that parallel the railway, but of course they have a lot more hills. The weather holds, and the scenery is magnificent: rivers, mountains, lakes, fields of purple lupine and yellow California poppies that dot the hillsides. We come across what looks like a golf course for cattle complete with sand traps and water hazards around the greens. Grazing cows munch their way along the fairways. We look down on this rangeland mirage from a high point on the road, resting after a couple of flat tires on the rough gravel. My flat is a ruptured valve site caused, I now believe, by tires being too highly inflated for the rough roads. When I reduce my pressure from 110 to 80 psi, the pressure recommended on the tire, I have only one ruptured valve (plus one puncture flat) on the whole remaining trip. The other flat that day on another bike is a pinch flat caused by being under-inflated. I am learning that a good tire gauge is an essential part of cycling gear.

After hours of bone-shaking gravel, we strike pavement and Granny M has a rear blow-out. It takes a couple of inflated tubes and repeated blow-outs to ascertain that the problem is a brake pad rubbing on her tire wall instead of the wheel rim. Another slipped piece of equipment on her bike. I sure hope this doesn't continue. She has to resort to a car ride into the bike shop at Princeton, and her chauffeur, Neil Anderson, turns out to be another cross-Canada, and even round-the-world cyclist who has also written books of his experiences. Neil and I have a lot in common. After he graciously transports the injured bike and its rider to the bike shop, he gives us some local tips along with his website address: www.cyclelogicpress.com. Neil's books and photography are an inspiration to all bike touring dreamers.

Jellicoe Station Inn is unrivaled, both in setting and hospitality. We are pedalling along a valley in the direction of the inn under increasingly menacing skies when a pickup passes, slows, and the driver yells out the window, "The Inn's van will meet you in about ten minutes up the road." The driver has seen us pause to watch newborn horses hobbling their first steps, and she knows the territory – and she has a cell phone. Suddenly the sky darkens and just as we reach the inn's four-by-four van with its bike trailer in tow, the rain starts. We quickly load for the crawl up a steep, rough road impossible to cycle. After about fifteen minutes of slow crunching and grinding, there, emerging from the treed mountain side, is a hand-built timber and stone house. We stow our bikes under the deck and enter a rambling array of rooms with polished marble and granite floors – even a bear skin rug. There are bedrooms and beds every which way, along with decorations and ornaments galore. Our hosts, Les and Darlene, are here to care for us: cold beer and a shellfish appetizer, salmon dinner with wild asparagus and home-made wine, respite from the rain. We are pampered. We break out a wee bottle of Courvoisier for a farewell tribute to Paul, who will leave us tomorrow. His law practice is too busy for him to get away for a longer period. But this is a beginning, he reassures us; he will be back for more. Someday.

This is the end of our first week. It feels like a month. Especially after another day of rough gravel roads that rattle and shake my shoulders and arms until they feel like they will fall off. No more rough stuff we tell ourselves. And we are in luck. There will be no more Trans Canada Trail, at least for a while.

The dynamics of our group begin living up to their reputation. Already there is a sense of loss as the second member of the group leaves us. Even though the first was with us only for a day, she held our final goodbyes in her hugs and kisses when we boarded the ferry. I think that forty-five kilometre ride to the ferry with our guide cushioned the impact of leaving more than we realized. Now the group has changed again; we are less one male, which leaves three women and one man. Up till now, the two men shared a motel room while we three women squeezed together, usually using a cot for a third bed. Not a lot of room to spare! We will still take turns sleeping with each other, but only two to a room means more space for us women, as well as more sleep for me. The two women are the loudest snorers of the group! But our departed man will be missed for his analytic chatter – everything was put into perspective in order to be fun. He could take things seriously – like getting the clamp fixed on Granny M's broken braze-on – but after he methodically found a machinist to do the job, he joked about his five dollar repair going across Canada (which happened until another fall required another clamping job several weeks later). Now, we ask ourselves, who will scout out the best places for dinner? He will be missed, and the group interactions will change.

Two weeks later he wrote in an email:

"I was so sorry to leave everyone in Summerland. I almost had withdrawal symptoms for the next ten days. I am so happy that you convinced me to do at least part of the trip and it was just unfortunate that my commitments were heavy at this time. I would really have liked to do all of B.C. ... I thought that we had just a great group and that everyone got along so well together. That helps to make the trip. It was a letdown to take Westjet from Kelowna to Victoria. We do 8 days of cycling to get to the Okanagan and Westjet took 55 minutes to get home. Those airline passengers don't know what they missed!

Over and above the company I look at it on two levels. On the macro side ... it is the freedom and clearing my mind of all of the day to day problems and issues I am responsible for and or worry about. And I am not a real worrier.... On the micro side of things I think I liked the satisfaction of knowing that I was able to do those hills! I feel cheated that I didn't get to do the rest of B.C."

Someday!

The rest of B.C. holds four more mountain passes: Anarchist between the Cascade Mountains and the Monashees at 1,233 metres; Blueberry-Paulson (also called Bonanza) between the Monashee and Selkirk Mountains at 1,535 metres; Kootenay between the Selkirk and Purcell Mountains at 1,774 metres; Crowsnest out of the Rocky Mountains on the Pacific/Atlantic Continental Divide and into the foothills on the B.C./Alberta border at 1,382 metres.

After a wonderful sunny ride south and mostly downhill along canals and lakes and rivers on paved roads or packed trails, and after passing through the wine capital of the Okanagan, we hole up in Osoyoos for a day off, our first! We have pedalled 612 kilometres in nine days – a foreshadowing of what lays ahead. Our view of the road switch-backing up Anarchist from our motel room on Osoyoos Lake is intimidating. We know it's going to take several hours to reach the summit, but can we ride it all the way? And what about the wind howling off the lake? A cyclist in town tells me the locals call the mountain the Antichrist – sounds more appropriate.

For some unknown reason, Monday is closing day for many Osoyoos businesses including the bike shop and the library for Internet. Thank goodness the Tourist Information Centre with computer access is open, and after a couple hours, I manage to create a Hotmail account to collect all my email addresses into one group address for my updates, something I couldn't make happen using my Telus account from home. Hotmail appears to be the way to go when travelling outside one's home base.

After all that time on the computer, I resort to self maintenance for my bike and I am not happy. I would like a good mechanic to give me a tune up and once-over. I have a slow leak in my rear tire – the one that hasn't had a flat – so I change my tube only to discover another wrecked valve that I cannot repair (no more 110 psi!); now I have no spare tube as the bike shops thus far have been out of stock for my size and valve type. Fortunately, another cyclist is carrying the same size and has one spare left. I'm not sure what our omen from Osoyoos is.

A big storm with high winds rattles our windows all night! We are reluctant to leave, but Grand Père checks with the locals at the motel and is assured the storm will decrease once we are away from the lake. And they are correct, at least about the wind. It dies in spurts, while the rain continues in spurts. We are encouraged after climbing twelve kilometres in the first two hours in only light showers. But two-and-a-half more hours and a total of thirty kilometres later we reach the summit sign – in the rain. I stop for a pee and bring up the rear to see Lynda standing at the roadside under an umbrella, like Mary Poppins. When I comprehend this bizarre picture, I wonder if I have worked too hard and am suffering a lack of oxygen to my brain.

I pedal forward and see a car parked in the ditch. It is Lynda's seventy-seven year old aunt, who lives nearby, who has come to meet us, complete with umbrella, pizza and homemade lemonade. She stresses the homemade! We squeeze our wet bodies into her car for a very welcome break and snack and warm-up. We are beginning to cool down after all the climbing, and from now on the downhills are cold! After another two hours including a lunch break and another warm-up, we check into a motel and just miss a downpour!

This has been quite a day – the Antichrist, Lynda "Mary Poppins" and her aunt, homemade lemonade, wind and rain and cold, Granny M's thirty-sixth wedding anniversary. In our motel room "Mary Poppins" produces more magic. This time it's hot chocolate laced with rum – a generous spoonful of sugar that soothes our aching bodies and warms our hearts. She will be leaving us soon and I'm already thinking about the new group dynamics. But first there are more mountains – and three more passes! We have been lucky to not have real snow, just a few flurries in the air. So far.

We pedal into Midway, which looks like the midpoint between the Alberta border and the Pacific Ocean on the map. We are now following Route 3, the main highway across southern B.C. and usually with a fairly wide shoulder. After a little climb up to Eholt Summit from Midway, I experience a first – a twenty kilometre grade of gradual descent that doesn't require braking – at all! This is the ride that makes it all worthwhile! The road travels a ridge above a river valley bursting with spring. There are lilacs and tulips, even a few fruit trees in blossom.

We are in Boundary Country, home of the gold rush in 1860. Later it was copper, then apples and potatoes. Doukhobors were some of the original settlers, and many still live here. One of their communes is now a museum we are told, but do not take the time to visit. I feel like I am cycling in my own commune, sharing motel rooms with whomever, pedalling with whomever, eating with anyone who happens to be around. Russian restaurants are popular in the area, but none of us care for the heavy fare. I am trying to stick to a healthy athlete's diet and am usually successful. Lots of carbohydrates. However, I am losing weight, which I don't want to happen too quickly or too much. Second breakfasts should put it back on, when I can make myself eat them.

Gold panning mural, Salmo

We stop for coffee (and high calorie goodies!) in Greenwood, a classic early mining and then agricultural centre with old store fronts that look like movie sets. Painted on the side of one tall brick building is a washed out sign for the "Strawberry Capital of the San Juans." Strawberries in the boundary area of the interior of B.C.? The waitress sets me straight. This is where the movie "Snow Falling on Cedars" (set in the San Juan Islands near Victoria, and a real strawberry capital) was filmed several years ago, as well as being the backdrop for other films. It is also where Lynda's father was born, she tells us as an aside. Another claim to fame is the nearby detention centre for Canadian Japanese interned during World War II, now marked by a stone monument on the edge of town, I am told. There is no snow falling at the moment, but it's cold enough. There are big hail storms north of us that we are tracking on the Weather Channel. We have cold wind, some spitting rain, some sun. And lots of cedars!

A two hour stop at a bike shop in Grand Forks allows Grand Père to replace his brake pads which have worn down to the metal, plus the mechanic does major adjustments for the brakes and derailleur on Granny M's bike. My trusty Trek 520 is standing me in good stead. I get my chain cleaned, a check-up, but still no spare tubes. But my tires are holding at 80 and 90 psi so I am reassured on all fronts! Lynda has her gears adjusted as well. We are halfway through the mountains, and she is halfway through her ride. A little nervousness seems to be creeping in, but we are sleeping better with only two to a room. We are all praying for the weather to hold. Or maybe even a little warmer, please God?

When we stop for lunch at a provincial park picnic spot, a warden asks the usual: Where are you heading? How long are you on the road for? Where have you come from? And so on. When he learns we are heading east, he smiles and shakes his head. "Well, Blueberry-Paulson is a life-changing experience! That's some climb! Good luck!" he yells to each of us as he drives away. I'm getting a little tired of the scaremongering over the passes. This is the route I have chosen, and everyone cycling with me has willingly agreed with it. We could be travelling further north on the TransCanada Highway, which would cut back on the number of passes, but we would still be crossing the mountains, and with a lot more traffic. So what's the big deal?

Well, Blueberry-Paulson is life changing. At 1,535 metres it is our second highest pass, but the steepest. After thirty kilometres to the summit, everyone is worn out! We collapse onto a huge construction bulldozer parked at the top, celebrating our triumph, daring the snow to really come down. And we are the scaremongers this time. A wee bit of hail along with only a few snowflakes ushers us onto a long sunny downhill, past mountain lakes with bits of snow on their shores amidst many cedars. A Super 8 Motel looms in our path, and within minutes we are in the hot tub. A wonderful reward! The whole day has been a big challenge, but we made it! The warden would be proud of us. And I think we are all feeling a little smug ourselves.

Towns disappear as we turn our maps to follow the route. Salmo takes the prize for murals with its rock mosaics inlaid by students of the Kootenay Stone Masonry Training Institute. They depict open pit mining, under-ground mining, and logging. We continue to dodge rain showers, watch for rainbows (good omens), and flirt with snow at higher elevations. Kootenay Pass is our highest point. We begin climbing in the morning at 9:30, and reach the summit

A snowy triumph!

by 1:00. We climb 1,000 metres in twenty-five kilometres of road. The sign at the top says we are 1,774 metres above sea level. Snow covers the ground around the lake and cariboo tracks crisscross the slopes. I didn't know this was cariboo country, and perhaps it won't be for much longer. Cariboo need one-hundred-year-old tree lichens for winter feed, and the old growth is being cut, so their food supply is disappearing. This is an example of the greed that can annihilate an ecosystem without a care. How much of this will I see on my bike ride across Canada?

The Kootenays are the most spectacular of all the mountains. Lost Creek ushers us up the pass with rushes of white water, trilium bloom through carpets of moss and pine needles, and brilliant red Indian paint brushes flash by at lower elevations. Most of what we see from our bikes is dense coniferous forest, but there are a few clearcuts as we leave the park. Mountain sheep leave their foot prints everywhere.

Go, Grandma, go!

After the snow-covered pass, down in the valley at the hamlet of Yahk, tall yellow arnica carpet a river bank – a sure sign of spring. I can't decide what the name "Yahk" is a sign of – other than those sure-footed beasts in the Himalayas that transport as well as feed and clothe the natives, or maybe rescue a mountaineer recovering from a near-by high-altitude adventure, similar to our own over the past few days. We stop in sunshine at Yahk for a picnic of hotdogs and ice cream – a total antithesis to our previous lunch stops – and it is only 12:30, so we decide to push on to Cranbrook. There's a very gentle climb along the river, but we hit our first headwind. Now we realize how lucky we have been as the wind has given us a push from behind (where it's supposed to be) prior to this. We set the record with our first century ride – 108 kilometres. It's twenty-five degrees Celsius, and the traffic has increased while road conditions have deteriorated. Rumble strips keep the traffic away from us, but make cycling hazardous. It's okay when the shoulders are wide enough, but when they narrow and the rumble strips take up the whole width, there is no choice but to ride on the road. The drivers are not considerate. This is our first encounter with nasty traffic, and in particular the truck drivers who would like to run us off the road.

From Cranbrook, we detour up to Kimberley for an R&R day at a friend's bed and breakfast. It is definitely a detour and a ride up – again – but Doug, our host bails us out with his car when he picks up our packs from the bike shop in Cranbrook. We find we have an easy pedal, much to my surprise. I knew the road was a climb, but after what we have ridden, it is nothing but a beautiful mountain back road. It's a piece of cake after one has spent the past three weeks traversing four mountain ranges!

A day off does wonders for my body and my soul. Our hosts treat us like royalty – cooking for us, giving us unlimited access to the Internet on Doug's computer, and providing laundry facilities. Walks in the woods, a drive to check out the ski hill – I don't even look at my bike for forty-eight hours (it was serviced in Cranbrook and again had nothing wrong with it). Helen, Doug's wife, has arranged an interview with the Kimberly Daily Bulletin and we all pose for their photographer; our photo and story will appear a few days after we leave. Granny M and I have had local newspaper coverage before leaving home, so this media attention is not new to us. If I can be an inspiration to other cyclists, I appreciate the publicity.

Lynda is more nervous as the days go by. Is it because she is almost finished? I have a déjà vu feeling as I have experienced this before with another friend who walked across England with me several years back. I will never forget her disquieting and increasingly disruptive behaviour, especially towards me, before she finally quit. I think she just couldn't complete the walk physically and didn't know how to quit graciously. I'm hoping our bike ride "between friends" is not the same scenario for Lynda and myself, but stress can play tricks on anyone. When her only flat tire happens on her last day, and when it is changed with aplomb by all of us in the rain, I think our mutual sympathies and assistance help. And I know that the end can be traumatic. There is this feeling of "what now?" I'm wondering what condition I'll be in after two and a half more months.

After we are revived by our day off, two days pass before another time-out, this one with husbands bringing good cheer plus camping gear along with spare tubes and a new tire to replace the spare used in the blow-out. We are now three continuing on across the rest of Canada. B.C. has been the preamble – the break-in – the physical conditioner. We've pedalled 1,287 kilometres over twenty-one days total. All those mountains and all that border-line weather is behind us. Now we are heading into summer in earnest, still following the lilacs at various elevations.

It's almost Victoria Day, our first national holiday of the trip. Snow is always a possibility at this time, but we are hoping to avoid any serious cold temperatures, especially as we will be camping. Shorts are the order of the day – until we wake to snow on the low mountains all around us as we make our final preparations. My load has increased with my camping gear, but my conditioning has also increased, so the extra weight doesn't feel too onerous. And thankfully the nervousness is left behind as we pedal down, away from the mountains. Once again, there are new group dynamics. Grand Père, Granny M, and myself carry on.

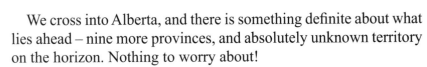

British Columbia

We cross into Alberta, and there is something definite about what lies ahead – nine more provinces, and absolutely unknown territory on the horizon. Nothing to worry about!

Logistics

We chose an early date for departure in B.C. to help beat the heat and humidity of eastern Canada later in summer, and to be ahead of the grasshoppers on the prairies. We knew we had risks of snow and cold in the mountains. We chose not to camp for this part of the ride, and we had winter clothing with us. We would begin camping in Alberta in a month when the weather would be more in our favor. An alternative camping route for B.C. is included at the end of this section.

The northern route versus the southern route through Manning Park: I chose the northern route to avoid Highway 3 through Manning Park, especially in late spring when a snow-covered slippery highway would be hazardous. Also, we all wanted to try and ride the Kettle Valley Railway (KVR) if possible. Distance-wise, the routes are about equal. Time-wise, we may have saved a day going south. Weather-wise, we had favourable weather on the northern route and probably would have had the same going south. If we had encountered snow on the KVR and our route became impassable, Coley Creek Lodge offered a 4x4 rescue service. After Coley Creek Lodge, we would use minor roads adjacent to the KVR if necessary.

Saturday, May 1 (day 1).

Ride: Victoria to Tsawwassen.
Follow Galloping Goose Trail to ferry terminal at Swartz Bay. (Ferry to Tsawwassen departs 3 p.m., 5 p.m., 7 p.m. – see www. bcferries.com) From Tsawwassen ferry terminal, ride south on

Boundary Bay Road 8 km to motel in Tsawwassen.

Facilities: All services including T.I. (trail maps for Galloping Goose) in Victoria and Sidney just before Swartz Bay. Bike shops in Victoria and Sidney.

Overnight: Night before at Admiral Inn, 257 Belleville St., Victoria (tel 888 823 6472), location a few blocks from Mile Zero marker in Beacon Hill Park. Lunch at Mattick's Farm on Galloping Goose Trail. Overnight at Beach Grove Motel, Tsawwassen (tel 604 943 2632).

Total distance: 52 km (actual Galloping Goose Trail Victoria to Sidney is approximately 40 km).

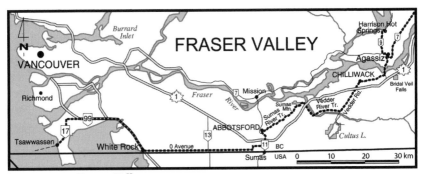

Route across Fraser Valley

Sunday, May 2 (day 2).

Ride: Tsawwassen to Abbotsford.
Follow Routes 17, 99, 99A to White Rock. To avoid congestion at border crossing, turn east at White Rock traffic light intersection on Rte. 99A with 8th Avenue and ride to 184th Street; then turn south to connect with 0 Avenue. Turn east on 0 Avenue and ride to Huntingdon Road near Abbotsford and continue east to junction with Route 11 (Sumas Way); turn north and cross under TransCanada Highway #1 to motel near intersection of Route 11 and TransCanada Highway.

Facilities: Lunch, groceries in White Rock. Best Western Bakerview Motor Inn, Abbotsford (tel 604 859 1341). Many restaurants in area, also groceries.

Total distance: 81 km.

Monday, May 3   (day 3).

Ride: Abbotsford to Harrison Hot Springs.
Follow Lower Sumas Mountain Road opposite Best Western Motel on Sumas Way about 5 km to Jensen Park where Sumas River Trail (part of Trans Canada Trail) begins. Stay on Sumas River Trail to join Vedder River Trail into Chilliwack. Trail is firm packed gravel. In Chilliwack ask for local directions to Pedal Sports bike shop if required. From bike shop there are minor roads connecting to Route 9 (Rosedale Highway) going north to Agassiz and crossing the Fraser River. From Agassiz follow signs to Harrison Hot Springs via Harrison Hot Springs Road going north. Consult TCT maps.

Facilities: Minter Gardens great lunch stop (access to cafeteria without paying entrance fee to gardens). Follow signs to Minter Gardens east of Chilliwack off Route 9. Bike shop in Chilliwack. Motels, restaurants, groceries in Harrison Hot Springs, also public hot springs pool.

Total distance: 77 km.

Tuesday, May 4   (day 4).

Ride: Harrison Hot Springs to Hope.
Follow Harrison Hot Springs Road south to Route 7; turn east on north side of Fraser River. Follow sign into downtown Hope and T.I. near the Dairy Queen (for latest information on KVR routes, closings, etc.). Be aware of logging trucks.

Facilities: Motels, restaurants, groceries, library, T.I. in Hope.

Total distance: 45 km.

Wednesday, May 5   (day 5).

Ride: Hope to Brookmere.
Follow Kawkawa Lake Road to Othello Tunnels (directions from T.I. in Hope). After tunnels, follow signs to Coquihalla Highway entrance 183. Coquihalla Summit at 1,244 metres is a few kilometres before toll booth. Exit at # 250 Larsen Hill. Head southeast and descend to river valley and onto wooden logging

bridge over river with very small sign for Trans Canada Trail and Brookmere. Coley Creek Lodge at Brookmere is on the KVR, approximately 10 km from Coquihalla Highway. Trail riding to Othello Tunnels and after highway; Coquihalla Highway to summit long and steep. Also steep 1.5 km up to Coley Creek Lodge. KVR is suitable for mountain bikes only.

Facilities: Restrooms at Coquihalla Highway toll booth. No food services on highway; carry food from Hope. Dinner, bed, breakfast, lunch for next day at Coley Creek Lodge; order supplies through lodge. www.coleycreeklodge.com.

Total distance: 91 km.

Thursday, May 6 (day 6).

Ride: Brookmere to Princeton.
Follow KVR for few kilometres to trail access at Aspen Grove Stage Road, which is gravel to Tulameen, then paved Coalmont Road to Princeton. KVR too rough for road bikes. Many hills on road.

Facilities: Tulameen good lunch stop. Restaurants, motels, groceries in Princeton. Bike shop in Princeton.

Total distance: 68 km.

Friday, May 7 (day 7).

Ride: Princeton to Jellicoe Station Inn.
Follow the KVR or ride paved Lake Osprey Summerland Road (Route 40) along Hayes Creek to the Inn's road opposite Chain Lake Campsite. Steep climb to the Inn; transportation provided.

Facilities: Take food from Princeton. Jellicoe Station Inn is B&B on KVR; arrange for dinner with reservations (tel 250 295 0160). Phone before leaving Princeton to give time frame for arrival at road junction where will be picked up.

Total distance: 48 km.

Saturday, May 8   (day 8).

Ride: Jellicoe Station Inn to Summerland.
Follow the KVR or Route 40 (Summerland Road) which becomes gravel after Osprey Lake (about 10 km from Jellicoe Station junction). Road is hilly and washboard rough.

Facilities: No services en route. Have snack food with you. Also lots of water. Motels, restaurants, groceries in Summerland.

Total distance: 60 km.

Sunday, May 9   (day 9).

Ride: Summerland to Osoyoos.
Follow Route 97 to Penticton and canal-side paved bike trail from bottom of Okanagan Lake to top of Skaha Lake – watch for right turn onto trail at canal. Ride to T junction, turn left and cross bridge to join the Old Highway on east side of Skaha Lake. Turn right and ride to Okanagan Falls, then rejoin Route 97 for about 10 km to right turn for Tuc-el-Nuit Drive just before McAlpine Bridge. Watch for road sign. Follow Tuc-el-Nuit Drive to T junction at Mt. Baldy Ski Road, turn left, then right almost immediately onto Black Sage Road that becomes unpaved river trail for short distance to Road 22 to Osoyoos. You are travelling through Oliver, the Wine Capital of the Okanagan. Road 22 connects to Route 97 into Osoyoos. Part of this route is used for the annual Iron Man Triathlon worldwide event. Lakeside trail through Oliver to Osoyoos winds past many wineries.

Facilities: Restaurants, wineries en route. Penticton and Osoyoos have all services. Bike shop in Osoyoos (closed on Mondays). Internet at Osoyoos T.I.

Total distance: 84 km.

Monday, May 10   (day 10).

Rest day.

Tuesday, May 11   (day 11).

Ride: Osoyoos to Midway.
Follow Route 3 over Anarchist Mountain. Summit at 1,233 metres takes about 4 hours.

Facilities: Lunch stop at Rock Creek Café. Overnight in Midway at Mile Zero Motel next to restaurant.

Total distance: 69 km.

Wednesday, May 12   (day 12).

Ride: Midway to Grand Forks.
Follow Route 3 through Boundary Country. Doukbhobor museum in Greenwood. Road is hilly, but no high passes.

Facilities: Copper Deal Cappuccino coffee shop/bakery on Main Street, Greenwood. Bike shop in Grand Forks. Motels, restaurants, groceries, T.I. in Grand Forks.

Total distance: 67 km.

Thursday, May 13   (day 13).

Ride: Grand Forks to Castlegar.
Follow Route 3 over Blueberry-Paulson (Bonanza) Pass. Steep climb to summit at 1,535 metres; allow three to four hours.

Facilities: Lunch stops at Christina Lake. Motels, restaurants, T.I., groceries in Castlegar. Super 8 Motel has free Internet access, hot tub and pool, breakfast included in room rate. Groceries near by, also Gabe's Restaurant.

Total distance: 95 km.

Friday, May 14   (day 14).

Ride: Castlegar to Salmo.
Follow Route 3 over Bombie Hill, a 6% grade up and down. Salmo famous for murals – can do short walking tour in town to see them.

Facilities: Take lunch from Castlegar. Overnight at SalCrest Motel on highway just before entrance to Salmo. (Motels in Salmo in poor condition.) Restaurant at motel. Library in town.

Total distance: 38 km.

Saturday, May 15   (day 15).

Ride: Salmo to Creston.
Follow Route 3 over Kootenay Pass. Spectacular mountain 3 to 4 hour climb to summit at 1,774 metres. Downhill steep and fast!

Facilities: Take lunch from Salmo. Motels, restaurants, groceries, T.I., library in Creston.

Total distance: 85 km.

Sunday, May 16   (day 16).

Ride: Creston to Cranbrook.
Follow Route 3 along river. Gradual up along river.

Facilities: Lunch stop in Yahk in park beside river. Gerick Sports Bike shop in Cranbrook. Cranbrook has all services; motels and restaurants on east side of town.

Total distance: 108 km.

Monday, May 17   (day 17).

Ride: Cranbrook to Kimberley.
Follow Wycliff Road and Route 95A. Ask locals for directions to Wycliff Road.

Facilities: Restaurants, motels, groceries in Kimberley. Westwinds B&B, Kimberley www.westwinds.ca.

Total distance: 33 km.

Tuesday, May 18   (day 18).

Rest day.

Wednesday, May 19 (day 19).

Ride: Kimberley to Fernie.
Follow Routes 95A to east on 3 which is two lanes with rumble strips on shoulders plus glass and debris and many trucks. Hills again, but no high passes.

Facilities: Lunch stop at Jaffray. Motels, restaurants, B&B's, groceries, T.I. in Fernie.

Total distance: 126 km.

Thursday, May 20 (day 20).

Ride: Fernie to Crowsnest Pass and Crowsnest Mountain Resort.
Follow Route 3 along Elk River to Sparwood and over Crowsnest Pass summit at 1,382 metres – a gentle climb. Cross Continental Divide at B.C./Alberta border.

Facilities: Lunch in Sparwood (detour off highway). Overnight at Crowsnest Mountain Resort, signposted on highway about 3 km before (west) town of Crowsnest, Alberta; resort has small cabins and restaurant. www.crowsnestmountainresort.com.

Total distance: 61 km.

Friday, May 21 (day 21).

Rest day.

Alternative camping route:

Central Victoria's closest to downtown camping spot is 11 km out at All Fun RV and Campground, 2207 Millstream Road, $18 for a tent site. This is the time to stay in a motel and get an early start for the ferry the next day.

White Rock is about 30 km from ferry dock. Parklander Motor Court with RV and tent sites, 16311 8th Avenue (tel 604 538 1727) is right turn (west) at 8th Avenue intersection with Hwy. 99 at traffic light in central White Rock.

Cultus Lake Provincial Park is a few kilometres south of Vedder River Trail intersection with Vedder Road in Chilliwack. There are two other campgrounds on the road before the park.

Harrison Hot Springs has full service camping at Harrison Hot Springs Camping and RV park in town. Hot pool and lake.

Hope Valley Campground, 62280 Flood-Hope Road, Hope, B.C. (tel 604 869 9857).

Brookmere has camping at Coley Creek Lodge, (tel 1 888 724 7799 or 604 869 9857).

Princeton Castle Resort & RV Park is on the Princeton-Summerland Road, 2 km from junction with Old Hedley Road and adjacent to the KVR.

Jellicoe Station has camping at Chain Lake Campsite and a B.C. Forest Service site. Approximately 40 km from Princeton.

Summerland has the Cedarbrook Campground, 5011 Hwy 97, near the Sun-Oka Beach on Okanagan Lake. Also Sun-Oka Beach and Kickiminee Provincial Parks.

Osoyoos: Hayes Point Provincial Park on Osoyoos Lake and Inkaneep Provincial Park on Hwy. 97 north of Osoyoos.

Midway/Greenwood: Boundary Creek Provincial Park is few kilometres east of Midway, near Greenwood.

Grand Forks has camping at the municipal campground in the City Park by the river.

Castlegar RV Park and Campground is 4 km west of town on Hwy. 3.

Salmo: Pine Springs Motel and Campground, 8 km west of Salmo on Hwy. 3 and Knights of Pythias Campground in town.

Creston: camping at Kozy RV Park and Campground on Hwy. 3 east, Pair-A-Dice RV Park and Campground in downtown Creston, Scottie's RV Park and Campground on Erickson Street, Creston.

Moyie Lake Provincial Park Campsite off Hwy. 3 approximately 85 km east from Creston.

Elko, about 90 km from Moyie Lake is Morrissey Provincial Park.

Alberta

License plate motto: Wild Rose Country
Official flower: wild rose
Official bird: great horned owl

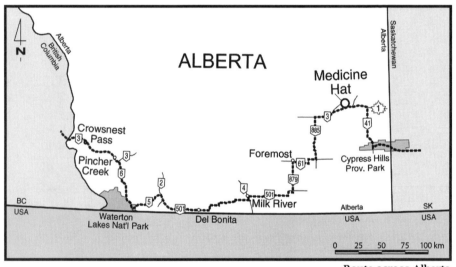

Route across Alberta

Saddle up and drive - or pedal -
Alberta's Cowboy Trail
		~ Cowboy Heritage Tourism

Highlights

B esides the definitiveness of facing the unknown, there is something else, almost unfathomable, about pedalling into a blank canvas that all the research in the world doesn't mitigate. It's what gets the adrenaline going; perhaps it's what gets me out here on my bike. Whatever it is, what lies ahead is different from grinds up known mountain passes in familiar scenery. Now it's roads I haven't driven, unknown terrain, the rest of Canada stretched out before me.

All I can do is pedal. Life is simple, stripped down to all I need for survival in the packs on my bike.

The weather does not look good. Crowsnest Mountain is trying to emerge through clouds but we don't see the peak all day. My day off is spent repacking and absorbing camping gear, and for a diversion, sightseeing at nearby Frank Slide Interpretative Centre. Its informative video on local history exposes the area's infamous bootlegging as well as the mining that undermined Turtle Mountain, creating the landslide that buried the town of Frank. The surrounding scenic areas offer hiking, fishing, mountain biking, snowmobiling and cross-country skiing in the winter, all those commodities that make the area ripe for development, and most likely for more ruination of the ever-shrinking wilderness.

Rain all night turns to light snow in the early morning, then a break with low clouds promises more moisture to come. We push off at 8:15, stop for breakfast with our departing husbands in the town of Coleman, and remount our trusty steeds. A quick good-bye avoids emotion. When will we see each other again? No one is asking. The tentative plan is for two-and-a-half months down the road. Time will tell. Grand Père is the man of the hour, a comfort to us grannies.

The rain resumes, a light drizzle at first, then heavier, and then snow! It's incredibly cold. Visibility is almost zero. Finally, there's a highway stop with a sign for a pizza shop. We slide under its overhang and dismount in stages. First, get both feet on the ground;

second, unwrap frozen fingers from the handlebars; finally, raise one stiff leg to clear the bike. We wipe our glasses to try and see, and then totter into the warmth of the shop. Grand Père is close to being hypothermic. His bare legs below his shorts are blue with cold. We all have numb fingers and toes. It takes a while to thaw out. Both Granny M and I have full rain gear covering our legs and feet, but it's still very cold.

My plan to ride south to Waterton Park and camp is scrapped. We will meet Grannie M's daughter's family at a motel in Pincher Creek, another forty kilometres down the road from our lunch warmup. They have come from Calgary for the holiday weekend and a final send-off for Grandma. The snow abates a little and we get to the motel by 2:00 p.m. under clearing skies but very chilly temperatures. Yes, they have rooms available for three shivering cyclists. At the entrance to town, rising like ghosts in the mist and snow, are larger-than-life wrought iron sculptures of cowboys and horses, a prelude of what's to come.

After a long hot bath, I think I can feel all parts of my body, but my toes are still tingly. A local Swiss restaurant serves a tasty fondue while we watch the now steady rain changing to intermittent snow. Obviously, we are going nowhere for at least another day. Grand Père acquires long waterproof pants from Granny M's son-in-law – a lucky fit for his six-foot-plus frame, and a necessary item for this weather. At the motel I find Internet access for a second email update to all those addresses I assembled in Osoyoos. I can tell that emails will be a time-consuming aspect of the trip, happening only on a day off. Lynda writes from back home:

"I am amazed that I could do it. I tried to get out of it, you know. [No, I didn't.] I even went to my doctor hoping he would say I couldn't do it. He thought it was a great idea! I was proud of myself for doing it, for being a good climber, for managing the aches and pains, but not for eating so much! I think I gave myself permission to eat what I wanted because I was so afraid of bonking, but I also hoped to lose more weight than I did. It was an experience – of physical endurance, of difficult relationships, and of not feeling in control of the situation. I saw it as your trip, and I was along for the ride, and sometimes that was hard."

Will we be friends when I get home? In terms of route planning,

Wind vane near Pincher Creek

this is my trip; I invited others to join me, and at the time, there were no objections to my proposed routes. However, one thing that is difficult to get across is that plans are susceptible to change and unknowns and uncontrollable circumstances such as weather and traffic and group dynamics. Now the group is reduced to only three musketeers, and we are forging ahead into unknowns big time! Will we all still be friends at the end?

I relish my unplanned down time. I realize I'm still tired from the previous strains of all those climbs in B.C. plus the recent winter conditions. An extra day's rest along with another long night's sleep is more needed than I had thought.

Finally, we are off. The sun is shining on a white world. Grandkids and their mom and dad blow kisses and call good wishes – our last connection with home. The three-year-old sings "Pedal on Grandma, pedal on," over and over. And so we pedal on....

Mountains meet the prairies abruptly – there are no foothills – and the route is spectacular! We are on the Cowboy Trail of Alberta, arguably one of the most beautiful cycling rides in the world. There are mountains covered with fresh snow in almost every direction as the highway rides a high ridge going straight south between the valleys. Twin Butte is the only town on the map for fifty kilometres between Pincher Creek and Park Gate at the entrance to Waterton

Park, and literally the only place to stop. The town's one and only building houses its post office, store, and a restaurant that serves the best huevos rancheros this side of Mexico. A few kilometres before Park Gate, we are greeted with a headwind coming up the cut from the lake, and Grand Père discourages us from doing the extra eight kilometres into the park. He isn't interested in one of the most famous views in Canada, where the lake and historic Prince of Wales Hotel are nestled in mountains that are undoubtly snow-covered. It is still early enough that we can make Cardston and a motel if necessary. It's still cool for camping, although we lose the snow almost as soon as we turn east.

I am disappointed to not see Waterton Park. It was high on my list to revisit after many years since my previous time there. I'm not sure why I let Grand Père make that decision for me, and I puzzle over the implications as I pedal on. Another beautiful ride! This is awesome biking country. Good roads, wide shoulders, and little traffic. The road rambles up and down gentle long hills into and around and out of coulees, their dry gulches sheltering birds, foxes, snakes, and sometimes a dry stream filled with spring runoffs that water even more wild creatures.

About ten kilometres out of Park Gate I have a broken spoke – the first in all my years of cycling! I'm just pedalling along and snap! Luckily it is on the front wheel. Grand Père frowns at my temporary solution of winding it around the next spoke, and at the next rest stop we take the wheel off and replace the snapped spoke with a spare I have brought with me. It is a time consuming operation, and after ninety-three kilometres we pedal into Cardston and straight to a motel with a hot tub and a restaurant. It's late; our warm daytime temperatures have dipped to the freezing point, and no one is enthused about camping. We are even less enthused when we learn the only grocery store is closed. There is no chance of a beer or glass of wine in this dry town. Its Mormon influence is reflected in its huge Alberta Temple visible on the hilltop above the town. There is a bike shop, but this is Victoria Day, and it too is closed. My front wheel is a bit wobbly, but after spending more time adjusting other loose spokes with my spoke tool, the wobbles appear to be cured. I will definitely check things out at the next available bike shop.

Our average speed is around sixteen kilometres per hour. I'm wondering if this is too fast, as most tourers agree that an average speed of twelve to fourteen kilometres per hour for a loaded touring bike is good time without over-exerting both body and equipment. But we all seem to be handling the speed okay, so I'm not complaining. Besides, so far we've been pushed by a prevailing southwest wind.

After my broken spoke, Granny M got stung by a bee below her left eyelid, just inside her sports-frame glasses. Grand Père was able to remove the stinger and there was only a little swelling. Curing the sting, and replacing a spoke make for two good deeds by my third cycling partner, but I'm still not sure about our route, and he is questioning my plans. We will hopefully reach Milk River by tomorrow night. This is another destination I have always wanted to visit, especially the petroglyphs at Writing-on-Stone Provincial Park, plus it leads to the road that will take us into the Cypress Hills. The map shows gravel roads, but a friend has told me most of the route is paved. One thing we have learned is that our narrow tires (Grand Père's are the skinniest) do not like unpaved roads. And how much I can trust friendly information from a casual cyclist remains to be seen.

Such a different world! The snow-covered Rockies perpetually loom behind us until we lose them after many kilometres, almost to Milk River. Then we are pedalling towards more snow-capped outlines on the horizon in front of us. The Cypress Hills? We are still several days away from the highest elevation between the Rockies and the east coast, so it's a possibility. But as we get nearer to Milk River, the hills disappear over the U.S. border to the south, and we swing a bit north.

Del Bonita is a border town where we stop for ice cream, the only "lunch" available at the only "town" between Cardston and Milk River, a distance of 115 kilometres. We lick our cones while resting in the shade of the town's two other stores that look permanently closed. This ghost town is on a popular cycling route from the U.S. that goes west to Waterton Park, then south to Glacier Park and over the Going to the Sun Road back to Kalispell, Montana. I hope those cyclists know to bring their own supplies for this section. Del Bonita – beautiful place – turns out to be the first of many isolated

and economically down-trodden stops on our route. I want to avoid the busy places and highways, but to have next-to-nothing as our only alternative is disconcerting.

When we turn north for five kilometres into the town of Milk River, the wind that has been chasing us suddenly hits from the side. It is almost impossible to pedal against the power that is broadsiding us. The Tourist Information (T. I.) is new and the people there are friendly; they point up the highway to a campground adjacent to the road. Pickups whip past, too close, throwing stones and dust and whirling debris in our faces. We are not encouraged. Shelley at the T. I. mentioned there are two motels in town; she also tells us the petroglyph guided walk at Writing-on-Stone Park will be at 10:00 and 2:00 tomorrow. It's about forty kilometres from Milk River town to the park – a good early morning's ride.

Curtains hang half on and half off the windows at the motel; a TV blares in the restaurant behind a haze of cigarette smoke. More pickups spin gravel in front of our rooms. The local weather channel quotes today's wind gusts at thirty-nine kilometres per hour; temperature at nineteen degrees Celsius. Our average speed for the day has been nineteen kilometres per hour with a maximum of sixty kilometres per hour. No wonder we covered the 115 kilometres in a little over six hours! We are beginning to understand the prairie winds – their strength and the importance of having them behind us.

Today has been a fantastic ride – I count eleven vehicles and two motor cycles in sixty kilometres – with many songbirds singing to us (warblers, killdeer, red-winged blackbirds, meadowlarks) and many ducks and pairs of Canada geese in low areas full of water. The road dips into coulees, with some upsides grabbing the climbing muscles, and others just a coast. This is a cyclist's paradise – if the wind is behind you!

We are pushed by the wind to Writing-on-Stone Provincial Park in time for the 10:00 guided tour into the petroglyph sites, only to find that the morning tours have not yet begun for the season. We can't wait for the afternoon tour unless we camp here for the night, and we do not have enough food with us. And no supplies are available at the campsite this early in the season.

Pedalling along the highway with its now familiar landscape of coulees and watering holes denies even a glimpse of the park until after the gateway and then a steep descent into a hidden river valley – surprise! This is a popular canoe launch for the Milk River as well as a secret hiding place for the Blackfoot Indians. As their sacred petroglyphs are well protected, we will not get to see them, but the hoodoos along the river banks are striking formations shimmering in the sun, worth a photograph at least. A red fox scurries from the ditch as I push back up; pronghorn antelopes are watching in the field. "No more petroglyphs," Grand Père mutters.

After 108 kilometres, half of them bucking a strong cross wind, we arrive at Foremost for our first night of camping. By the time we buy groceries and make a pharmacy stop, everyone in town knows we are here. "Where are you going? Where have you come from? How many kilometres today?" The usual. Then a woman at the bank warns us that the road east to Cypress Hills from Manyberries – tomorrow's ride – is indeed gravel, and possibly not yet open for the season. This is not good news. We have come this far south to see Waterton Park, which we haven't seen; likewise for the petroglyphs. We've had a good tailwind going east, but it will be a troublesome side wind when going north, the direction for most of our ride tomorrow. My at-home research on Cypress Hills told me I wanted to go there, but I could only find vague answers as to how to get there. Now I know. I ponder my map while enjoying a beer plus a hot rice and tuna casserole, à la campstove. There is no choice except going north to Medicine Hat, which I knew would be the alternative if we couldn't get through staying south, but now the alternate route is not appealing to anyone.

The campsite is part of a small municipal park near a major road on the edge of town. I watch as huge water-tank trucks fill at a well in the park's parking lot on their way to the local oil fields. Just before town we passed a few pumpers bobbing up and down, like the grasshoppers or rocking horses they are named after. I've heard a lot of discussion about water consumption by the oil and gas drilling industry. Now I'm seeing it. But at least Foremost isn't a ghost town – yet – perhaps thanks to the liquid gold gurgling under its foundations, plus its current water supply.

A woman playing with her toddler at the playground next to our tents and cooking shelter asks if we have discovered our feathered neighbors. When we plead ignorance, she shows us two baby great horned owls perched in the fir trees near the swings. The young ones are almost adult size at about forty centimetres tall, immobile high up near their nest. Magpies are hovering, and mamma is keeping a watchful eye from lower branches. New life – will the young owls make it?

Despite the wind, threatening rain, trucks, and the local birds, I sleep peacefully, a relief from the usual snoring in my ears, until 2:00 a.m. when a sudden wind storm rattles my tent. There are a few drops of rain. Next thing I hear is a cacophony of bird sounds. It's 4:00 a.m.! Magpies are harassing the owls, owls are hooting, crows cawing, finally other songbirds start. Just when I'm drifting into a little more sleep, my fellow campers start rustling about. My tent feels like ice! Juice, muffins, yogurt and fresh fruit revive me. One thing we don't worry about is refrigeration for our food. By 8:00 there are hints of warm sunshine and we are off.

There's a good tail wind until we turn north at Etzikom, which is another surprise. We stop for rhubarb pie and ice cream at the small hamlet's windmill museum and chat with Len, who assures us, maps and all, that once we get to Cypress Hills from Medicine Hat, we will be able to cycle across the hills into Saskatchewan. This is good news as the stretch of the TransCanada Highway from Medicine Hat east to Swift Current is mostly two lanes and notoriously dangerous

Etzikom Wind Power and Pioneer Museum

for vehicles, let alone cyclists. I don't want to ride it if I don't have to. I have talked with other cyclists who have done it and they have not given good reports. If I can get through Cypress Hills, I can stay south, closer to the U.S. border, and visit Saskatchewan author Sharon Butala's (*The Perfection of the Morning*, HarperCollins, 1994; *Old Man on His Back*, HarperCollins, 2002; *Lilac Moon*, HarperCollins, 2005) Old Man On His Back natural grasslands conservation reserve. There isn't much native grassland that hasn't been destroyed by the plow, and I want to see it. I have contacted Sharon regarding possibly connecting with her at her ranch near Eastend, and we have a tentative rendezvous arranged.

"Windmills of my mind" – what's that song? I think it goes "like the circles that you find, in the windmills of your mind." I have circled through windmills in my mind as I've pushed to Etzikom, zigzagging up long coulee uphills when there is no traffic. Pronghorn antelopes pranced across endless range land, jack rabbits paused, quails fluttered, and Canada geese flew in a V overhead. Now, at the Etzikom Wind Power and Pioneer Museum, besides the pie and ice cream and Len, there are windmills of every description, the most astounding one being a replica of an early Dutch two-story model. It has been transported here piece by piece by Len and his wife from Martha's Vineyard off the Atlantic coast of Massachusets in the U.S. – a true labour of love – and a reminder of my twirling mind. I'm still hoping we don't have to backtrack once we get to Cypress Hills, which I am very much looking forward to seeing.

Dutch windmill,
Etzikom Wind
Power and
Pioneer Museum

Medicine Hat is a collision with my windmills. We have been told to take Route 120 from Seven Persons as a cutoff to the southeast side of the city and motel row. We then come face to face with the TransCanada Highway, our first major traffic confrontation of the whole trip. It is a shock! We get ourselves across several divided lanes and into the nearest Comfort Inn where air conditioning drowns the traffic noise. I know there's a campsite somewhere in the city, but no one mentions camping. It's been a 123 kilometre day with an average speed of twenty kilometres per hour – one of our longest and certainly our fastest yet.

Cyclepath Bike Shop is easy to find, and I am happy to get a tune-up and my wheels trued, but not so pleased to hear I will probably have more broken spokes due to the age of my bike and the brittleness of my spokes. This will be especially true for my front wheel that has alternating loose and tighter spokes (that spokes weaken with age is apparently common knowledge although news to me). Broken spokes are a touring cyclists number one problem, according to the mechanic. Since spokes support touring loads while keeping the wheels in alignment, I know they can make or break a ride. I am faced with buying new or rebuilding my old wheels, or I can try shifting some weight to the rear and hope for the best. As this is the first broken spoke of my entire biking career, it's not difficult to make the decision. I buy six more spokes to replenish my supply, rearrange my panniers, and hope for the best. My rear wheel appears to be okay – no loose spokes despite carrying more of the load, although I had my heaviest items (tools, toiletries, camp stove and fuel) in the front. Hopefully, shifting some weight will make a difference.

Grand Père goes full-out for a new cogset and chain plus a new saddle. Along with a tune-up, Grannie M has the C clamp on her rear rack reinforced (it had slipped again and was rubbing on her chain), her headset tightened, and new rear brake pads (a more elongated version to replace the already worn ones replaced after her blow-out). Once again, we are as mechanically sound as we can be. Eight more provinces to go, once we get out of Alberta.

Cypress Hills is east for twenty kilometres on the four lane divided TransCanada Highway and then forty kilometres on a two lane road going south and up. We climb almost 1,000 metres, the last twenty kilometres in cold rain and a strong headwind – worse than Pincher Creek because of the climbing. At least there is no snow. Our average speed is fourteen kilometres per hour – a bit different from yesterday! Everyone is exhausted.

At Elkwater there's a cabin with three beds in two bedrooms plus a living room available for $110. It's warm and dry! We walk to a restaurant down on the lake. Wild turkeys display their plumage; yellow-headed blackbirds sing in the rushes on the lake shore. There's a hint of a colourful sunset until icy showers and even some hail wipe out the horizon. Please, no more snow, is my only request to the weather gods!

Despite being Canada's only interprovincial park, no one we meet in Cypress Hills, Alberta knows anything about Cypress Hills,

Frenchman River Valley

Saskatchewan. Even the maps at the wardens' office stop at the border between the two provinces. And no one knows if the roads are passable. One thing that is agreed upon is that the roads are not paved. So much for Len's guiding remarks (he even showed me on a topographical map the roads he claimed were paved, "except for maybe a kilometre or two," he had said). Our only recourse is to backtrack to the formidable Highway #1 that becomes two lanes and scary at the Saskatchewan border.

Grand Père wonders if there isn't someone with a pickup who could drive us through the hills to Fort Walsh, Saskatchewan where we could get onto pavement to go south via Maple Creek. He isn't happy about first going north, then south, and now back-tracking again. And of course neither am I.

During my research at home, I consulted with a Regina native who "knows southern Saskatchewan like the back of my hand." He assured me, again with maps at hand, that following my southern route would be most enjoyable with small towns and friendly people, easy terrain and little traffic. Now we just have to get there!

It's Saturday and the wardens' office is technically closed – just my luck – but there are two staff inside who respond to my knocking. They both agree that they should know more than they do about the other half of their park, and listen patiently to my complaints. The lack of information combined with difficult weather have put three cyclists in an awkward position. Finally, they have an idea. Maybe Phil can help us – if he is around. Phil is a park employee and firefighter, so his whereabouts are not predictable, but Tessa down at the Visitor's Centre may know where he is. As I'm walking down to the centre, the woman from the wardens' office stops to offer me a lift. She and Tessa agree that Phil may be a quick phone call away. He's been seen in the area just yesterday. They call his home, tell him our predicament, and he tells them he may be able to help. This is sounding almost too good to be true. The woman with the park vehicle takes me up the road a few blocks to his house. Hair wet and shiny from the shower, he greets me with a mischievous smile. It's his day off, but the prospect of helping stranded cyclists is enticing. All he has to do is put fluid in his radiator and some air in his tires, and he's ready to go. "Give me an hour," he says.

I pass an old orange pickup resting on four half-flat tires behind his house on my walk back to our cabin. The single cab has one bench seat. That must be it, but I don't tell the others about the truck's condition. Thumbs up, I say! My cycling buddies settle into vintage Casablanca on TV; I finish packing and wander outside in search of wild turkeys. They are hiding. I watch the back end of the old pickup ease around the corner towards the gas station, and cross my fingers.

Phil is an inspiration. He is an Helitack Firefighter in Cypress Hills (and ultimately in all of Canada and the U.S.) and also teaches during the winter at SIAST, the Saskatchewan Institute for Applied Science and Technology, in Prince Albert, Saskatchewan, which is "ultimately" 700 kilometres to the north. I call him Mr. Ultimately as ultimately is his favourite word. And ultimately he gives us the ride of our lives. A native of Montréal, just like Grand Père, he was lured west looking for employment and found his niche, first as a ranch hand and then with the fire fighters. He has worked on both sides of Cypress Hills and knows the area well. Whether the '79 Dodge pickup he bought for $1,000 from a rancher he used to work for will get us across the border into Saskatchewan in anybody's guess. The truck has been christened La Vielle Citrouille, The Old Pumpkin, by two French Canadian women he rescued from a drenched campsite last year, so these expeditions are not new to the truck or its driver.

Cypress Hills is an "island in the ice" according to the sign at Reesor Lake Lookout. The "island" is the top one hundred metres of a plateau originally formed by erosion, and then left untouched by advancing glaciers that surrounded the plateau. It is the highest point between the Rocky Mountains and Labrador, which is ultimately difficult to believe. Elkwater and our last night's cabin at 1,274 metres is just a little higher than the Coquihalla summit in B.C., but this is not the mountains. I don't feel like I'm at elevation as Phil maneuvers La Vielle Citrouille around and through puddles and minor washouts on saturated boggy gravel roads that bisect relatively flat lodgepole pine forests. Some road blocks are up and our guide is hoping he remembers where to go. This, indeed, is an adventure!

I take photos of white pelicans on Reesor Lake. I have never seen a white pelican. Other bird life is equally phenomenal. Eagles soar overhead, and a lone moose munches a tree as we slip past. We come out at Maple Creek on a paved road in Saskatchewan! There is a very nice resort at Fort Walsh where we head for lunch. This is a treat. When I tell Phil I am hoping to meet with Sharon Butala at the Old Man On His Back conservation area, he immediately knows who and where I'm talking about and offers to continue with us as far as Eastend, where he will visit an old friend from his ranching days. We drive along the Davis Creek Road through afternoon sun bouncing off multicoloured buttes layered with white mud that has been mined for pottery clay over many decades. White Mud is another name for the Frenchman River that snakes through a moonscape of buttes and cliffs. Ultimately, Phil takes us up onto Jone's Peak for a lookout over the valley. The view is breathtaking, as are the ruts and mini lakes we grind through to get up the steep hill. The wind is ferocious but there's no more rain. An old man on his back is outlined on the horizon.

Phil drops us at the campground in Eastend, unfortunately located across the river from the *T.rex* Discovery dinosaur museum built into a hillside and above the excavations of local prehistoric remains. La Vielle Citrouille's radiator hasn't overflowed and the tires are still inflated. Phil refuses any payment for our adventures, and we are glad we at least bought him lunch. He heads for town; we search for shelter from the wind and probable rain to come. We erect our tents amongst budding trees and shrubs just breaking into leaf. This is definitely early in the season. We can't get across the river to the museum before it closes, and so head to town for groceries instead. Not saying much, each of us contemplates our miraculous rescue by a truly (and ultimately) remarkable rescuer. No one suggests we cheated by hitching a ride. And I'm very happy I didn't have to ride that narrow stretch of TransCanada #1 to get here! I place a call to Sharon Butala and leave a message – she isn't available. I'll call back if possible.

We are in Saskatchewan! We've pedalled 559 kilometres over the past six days.

Logistics

Mountains dropping into prairies – cowboys, petroglyphs, famous parks – dreams of little traffic and good roads on an unknown cycling route. Will these dreams come true? What does the weather hold in store for us? The route goes south before turning east: first Waterton National Park of Canada, then Writing-on-Stone Provincial Park of Alberta, then Cypress Hills  Interprovincial Park connecting through to Saskatchewan.

Saturday, May 22 (day 22).

Ride: Crowsnest Pass to Pincher Creek (motel).
Follow Route 3 turning south at junction with
Route 6.

Facilities: Lunch stop at Lundbreck. Motels, restaurants, groceries at Pincher Creek. Parkway Motel on Route 6 on west side of town (turn left at intersection before town centre), Swiss restaurant nearby. Most stores and restaurants closed on Sunday.

Total distance: 58 km.
Average speed: 17 kph.
Maximum speed: 49 kph.

Alternative Camping:
Pincher Creek: Pincher Creek Veterans Memorial Park & Campground; Sleepy Hollow Campground. Waterton: Waterton Townsite Campground; Crooked Creek Campground 5.6 km east of Park Gate on Hwy 5; Waterton Riverside Campground 5 km east of Park Gate on Hwy 5.

Sunday, May 23   (day 23).

Rest day (snowing).

Monday, May 24   (day 24).

Ride: Pincher Creek to Cardston (motel).
Follow Route 6 to Park Gate, then east on Route 5, the Cowboy Trail of Alberta to Cardston. Good roads, wide shoulders, little traffic, rolling ranch land.

Facilities: Lunch stops at Twin Butte and Mountain View. Motels, restaurants, groceries in Cardston (no alcoholic drinks).

Total distance: 93 km.
Average speed: 16.5 kph.

Alternative Camping:
Cardston: Lee Creek Campground.

Tuesday, May 25   (day 25).

Ride: Cardston to Milk River town (motel).
Follow Route 501 southeast out of Cardston. Gently rolling terrain on good road with wide shoulder.

Facilities: Only stop en route is Del Bonita for snacks and ice cream. Motels, restaurants, T.I. in Milk River.

Total distance: 115 km.
Average speed: 19 kph.
Maximum speed: 60 kph.

Alternative Camping:
Milk River Municipal Park.

Wednesday, May 26   (day 26).

Ride: Milk River town to Foremost Municipal Park campground.
Follow Route 501 east to Writing-on-Stone Provincial Park, then north on Route 879 to Foremost. Ask local directions to

municipal park. Watch for gophers running in front of bikes. Shoulders usually adequate, traffic is sparse, rolling ranch land.

Facilities: No services between Milk River and Foremost. Scheduled petroglyph tours at Writing-on-Stone Provincial Park (check with park rangers for times); hoodoo volcanic rock formations at park. Groceries, bank, pharmacy, liquor store in Foremost.

Total distance: 108 km.
Average speed: 18 kph.
Maximum speed: 50 kph.

Thursday, May 27 (day 27).

Ride: Foremost to Medicine Hat (motel).
Follow Route 61 east to Route 885 north at Etzikom to Route 3 east to Seven Sisters; turn right onto Route 120 and watch for left turn towards Medicine Hat after about 15 km (before junction with TransCanada #1); ask for local directions to avoid downtown Medicine Hat. Wind Power and Pioneer Museum and lunch/snacks at Etzikom. Long coulees, good roads.

Facilities: All services in Medicine Hat. Cyclepath and other bike shops in Medicine Hat.

Total distance: 123 km.
Average speed: 20.5 kph.
Maximum speed: 52 kph.

Alternative Camping:
Medicine Hat: Wild Rose Trailer Park and Campground (ask local directions); Cavan Lake Campground 20 km east & 5 km south off #1.

Friday, May 28 (day 28).

Ride: Medicine Hat to Elkwater, Cypress Hills (motel).
Follow TransCanada #1 east to turn south on Route 41. Cypress Hills rise 600 metres above surrounding plains. Bird life outstanding, also antelope and small rodents, wild turkeys at Elk Water.

Facilities: No services Medicine Hat to Cypress Hills. Take lunch from Medicine Hat. Overnight at cabin at Elkwater Green Tree Motel, restaurant on lake in Elk Water. Warden station near motel.

Total distance: 62 km.
Average speed: 14 kph.
Maximum speed: 44 kph

Alternative Camping:
Several campgrounds in Cypress Hills park.

Saturday, May 29   (day 29).

To Eastend Municipal Campground, Saskatchewan via hitch-hiking.

Facilities: Lunch at Fort Walsh. Restaurant, groceries in Eastend. Also Stegner House, local pioneer museum, *T.rex* Discovery Centre.

Alternative ride would be cycling 80 km Medicine Hat to Maple Creek for overnight camping at Deer Hollow Tent Campground in Maple Creek or several campgrounds located 28 km south of Maple Creek on Hwy 21 near Cypress Hills Provincial Park, Saskatchewan; then ride 80 km to Eastend for overnight camping at municipal park, thus avoiding Cypress Hills.

Alternative # 2: Continue on The Cowboy Trail of Alberta, Route 61, after Cardston to Etzikom, thus avoiding Milk River and Writing-on-Stone Provincial Park. (See May 27, Thursday, for Etzikom to Medicine Hat.) These routes also avoid busy Lethbridge. Camping available at Raymond, Alberta on Route 61.

Saskatchewan

License plate motto: Land of Living Skies
Official flower: western red lily
Official bird: sharp-tailed grouse

Route across Saskatchewan

*These prairies begin to impose their awful
perfection on the observer's mind.*
~ Wallace Stegner, *Wolf Willow*, 1955

Highlights

Eastend, Saskatchewan, on the Red Coat Trail. Population around 1,500. Wide dusty streets crisscross to form this once eastern-most outpost of the Mounties in western Saskatchewan. Insignificance is my first impression, but I know there's more to this place than a dusty nondescript townsite. There's the dinosaur museum; Pulitzer Prize-winner Wallace Stegner has also left his mark. In Stegner's book *Wolf Willow*, first published in 1962, he tells of his growing up in the area, as well as relating the history of the Mounties and Indians who long inhabited the Frenchman River Valley and Cypress Hills. Wolf willow, a prairie shrub that's commonly found along river banks, gives off a particular sweet smell in the spring. Ultimately, the smell is one of Stegner's fondest memories. We are probably too early for wolf willow, but lilacs are blooming in a few windswept yards – an encouraging sign.

I find the side street to the Stegner House and photograph an early 1900s home surrounded by newly mown lawn. I know the house is maintained by the Eastend Arts Council as a residence for artists; it is small and old and looks oddly comfortable, especially the enclosed front porch – an ideal place to write a book about a bike ride across Canada. Hmmm!

My cycling buddies are less impressed. Grand Père is not interested in dinosaurs or local writers or seeing the grasslands at Old Man On His Back. Sharon Butala has mentioned to me that the dinosaur museum sometimes takes people out to the conservancy land; I should check with them. When I mention this to my partners, there are objections, the first being that Butala could not possibly be available as she is presenting a writing workshop on the west coast that Lynda's husband is attending. I know the workshop is soon, but did not realize it coincided with our hoped-for arrival at Eastend, which my partners are sure is the case from their conversations with Lynda. So I do not phone Sharon back, and I give up seeing her conservancy grasslands. Another of my raison d'être for this part of the trip squelched.

Sharon writes an email that catches up to me several days later saying she was just out for the afternoon when I phoned, and that we could have touched bases after all. Her workshop wasn't for another couple of weeks. But I don't know this at the time of course; I just listened to negative reactions from my partners. I try to maintain my cool, but when I get the clarifying email from Sharon I am truly angry, mostly with myself for listening to others when I should have known better. But for now we are all innocent, and I tell myself to agree with my partners and just get riding. No more sidetracking, which suits the others just fine! I know that exploring southwestern Saskatchewan is my own personal agenda, but hoped I could get the others to agree. Obviously, this is not going to happen. I am learning the art of compromise on a bike ride with partners who do not share aspirations or priorities similar to my own. And I still have a long way to pedal!

Snap, crackle, pop. More snapping, footsteps, crackles, sparks flying in red shadows, twigs breaking, crunch. I rub my eyes, raise up on my elbow. I must be dreaming – this is a scene from *Star Wars* – outside is red night being whipped by the wind. It's circling around my tent. Snap, breaking twigs, footsteps very close. Someone has started a fire – in gale-force winds! I watch as red swirls in the sky outline a human figure that bends and snaps, stoops and breaks twigs, scoops and grabs while scouring the ridge a few steps above my tent. I stay put. Besides the fire crackles and spits, there are voices. Some kids must be having a spring fling. But don't they realize it's too windy to torch the dry winter dead-fall in this campground? I watch, and wait, and take deep breaths. It seems like half the night later before the shadows disappear, and feet stop crunching around my tent. Hopefully their beer has run out and they'll go home – anywhere other than here. So much for quiet southwestern Saskatchewan camping!

The others haven't heard the fire, or the wind, or the footsteps and voices. Maybe I really was dreaming. But for them, night noises are not an issue. Granny M doesn't hear them and Grand Père ignores them. Daytime is different, and now for all of us the wind becomes a major force to be reckoned with. As long as it's behind us, we

Camping,
Eastend

make great time, but turning across or into it threatens to delete
any gains, or even defeat us completely. Quoting Stegner from the
1950s: "You don't get out of the wind, but learn to lean and squint
against it." Nothing's changed, except it's more difficult to lean
and squint against it on a bike. And just our bad luck, its direction
today is not the usual southwest, but from the northwest.

It's on our back quarter for the first forty kilometres to Shaunavon,
a more prosperous town with a pretty municipal park and campsite
in its centre, and giant signs at the road junction commemorating
its famous hockey players. Between the wind and hockey players,
we cannot forget we are on Canadian prairies! Today is Sunday
– grocery stores are closed, and it's too early to stop. We turn north,
cross-wise to the wind for ten kilometres of turning pedals at a
turtle's pace. The angle of my bike is alarming; I'm remembering
being blown off my bike in Scotland a few years back. There I was,
eye-to-eye with the sheep, handlebars askew, front packs splayed
off to my side and unnoticed by the grazing wooly bundles that
politely stepped around me and my strange accoutrements. I look
where I'd end up if the same mishap happened here. The ditch is
wide and wet and no doubt full of prickly burs for my bare legs.
Better than sheep droppings? I ask myself, chuckling, obedient to
advice from the pros: divert your mind, sing, laugh, do something
ridiculous. Is holding on against this wind ridiculous enough?

We must make a weird picture. One man stops to ask where we are going, and so on. Obviously he can't resist stalling us in our struggles, but I can't stand it. Ahead I can just see a sign with a Mountie's head. I inch away from the windbreak of the car and after a few minutes that seem like an eternity, I turn east. I'm on the Red Coat Trail again. The wind is behind me. Whew!

Wheat fields swirl in every direction, stretching into infinity. We zoom past a domestic bison herd, roadkill badgers as big as coyotes, and almost beyond the few buildings of a town called Cadillac before we stop. There's no way this dot on the landscape remotely resembles a Cadillac. What was I expecting? There are some people gathered outside a large Quonset hut that turns out to be an indoor equestrian arena. It's even too windy outside for horses. The locals confirm our suspicions – yep, that's the campsite in the field across from the horse barn. There's probably water from that standpipe over in the corner under that lonely tree, that's the outhouse down the track over there. Best to go on to Ponteix where there's a motel and restaurant. "It's a blowin' out here," they remind us.

This motel routine is getting too familiar. It's stretching our budget; we are ready to camp. Ponteix is another dusty mini town with boarded-up shops. But it has a decent motel, complete with a deep-fry restaurant across the road. I photograph a mural depicting the town's French heritage; grain elevators glimmer in evening light. The lady at the motel tells us not to miss the church, surprisingly hidden from sight until we climb a slight hill on a back street to be confronted by an enormous red brick edifice with high twin steeples. The Notre Dame d'Auvergne. Grand Père wonders if Ponteix comes from the Auvergne region in France. If so, the French mountainous counterpart is the complete opposite to this outpost in rural, isolated, flat Saskatchewan – except for its church. I wonder what those immigrants thought when they got off the train. One thing I'm sure of – the wind was blowing!

Almost 100 kilometres east of Ponteix at the town of Gravelbourg is the terminus of the railway that delivered thousands of French Canadian Catholic families from eastern Canada to these farm lands in the early 1900s. Gravelbourg's hand-painted cathedral, now a National Historic Site, is a kind of memorial to the early settlers, and even Grand Père wants to see this famous landmark.

At sixty kilometres per hour the wind is too strong. It's difficult to maintain equilibrium on the bike, let alone have adequate control. In three hours and twenty minutes we cover seventy-two kilometres, average speed twenty kilometres per hour! I'm ready to quit; Grand Père thinks it's wonderful until he faces the prospect of turning north, across the wind, for the last twenty kilometres to Gravelbourg. There's a campsite about five kilometres from the intersection with the northbound road, if we can make it that far. I'm wondering if we could then just hitch a ride to see the cathedral while waiting for the wind to calm down.

We are almost at the intersection with what looks like a few facilities in a small town when a blue van stops, a window rolls down, and someone yells "Are you ladies from Canmore, Alberta?" The wind is playing tricks, whisking strange words through the air.

Ponteix,
Saskatchewan

Our Lady of
the Assumption
Co-Cathedral,
Gravelbourg

I cross the road and recognize the driver. We had met in Canmore just before I left and joked that we might see each other on the road, as she was making a trip to Ontario somewhat within my time frame. But now, connecting in the middle of rural Saskatchewan is a bigger miracle than Lynda's Mary Poppins roadside umbrella in B.C.! Ruthie offers to help in any way possible, and it doesn't take long to figure out that we can take turns using her van to ferry us up to Gravelbourg. A woman at our earlier breakfast stop told us about Heritage Place B&B, a conversion of a former field house for men and women of Catholic faith who wanted to live simply and serve others. "It's an inexpensive retreat from the elements,"

she smiled. Yeah, right, another escape. I smiled back. "Good to know. Thanks." Now I'm grateful for the information, and for our rescuer.

We pedal up to a parking space near the intersection and load two bikes, all the packs, and myself in the back of the van for the first trip. Just before the left turn into town is the B&B, within walking distance of the cathedral, if we can stand up against the swirling force that wants to flatten everything in its path. Later, by the time we all settle into the B&B, the wind drops and we become tourists.

The cathedral's construction was an astonishing feat completed in 1919 with a Michelangelo touch. Monsignor Charles Maillard, the resident priest at the time, spent the next ten years painting the interior walls with Biblical scenes that are remarkably well preserved. The current priest tells us the stained glass windows came from France as did the historic bishop's chair that dates from the 1700s. The bishop's home next door is almost as grand as the cathedral.

Today's Gravelbourg has one of the only French secondary schools in western Canada – completely French and not a variation of English with French immersion courses. Our B&B hosts, MaryLynne and Walt, have a son at the school. The whole family is a working advertisement for this town of 1,200 dubbed "A Touch of Europe on the Prairies." MaryLynne has won awards for her contribution to historical research as well as tourism in the area. We cyclists are invited to attend that evening's community pot luck supper in honour of the retiring priest. Homemade hospitality! I pass on the dinner in favour of MaryLynne and Walt's computer hospitality to get caught up on emails and write another of my updates, which are becoming few and far between.

Clouds and less wind greet us in the morning. We leave the lilacs and tulips and irises blooming in Gravelbourg to pedal east and then south for most of the day. The landscape is an endless prairie of wheat. A couple of startled pronghorns, heads up, ears alert note our passing. There are lots of ducks and geese and loons in the water holes. A stop at Assiniboia's Tourist Information Centre tells us that my original idea of camping at St. Victor's Petroglyphs Provincial Park is a good one, and Route 2 going south to the park turnoff is a quiet road. We soon find out why. It is our first encounter with truly rough road conditions. It's about ten kilometres of rough stuff before the turnoff for the park, which is another eighteen kilometres on what appears to be a good paved road into the campsite. The road coming out the other side of the park is gravel, which means we would have to backtrack on pavement in the morning – after seeing the petroglyphs. I should have known. Grand Père scoffs at the hypotheses that explain petroglyphs and does not want to go into and back out of the park in order to camp. The map and my research show nothing for camping until Big Beaver, another 100 kilometres down the road. We've already clocked sixty on the cyclometre, and it's getting late. The rough roads plus a four kilometre walk through fields around road construction in the morning have slowed us down. But maybe there's a motel at one of the towns on the way, or a campsite I don't know about. We pedal on. Looks like I am not going to see petroglyphs on this trip unless I fight for them.

We manage a surprising twenty kilometres per hour average speed for the day's total of 123 km. There's a seedy-looking motel at Rockglen; we scrounge a similarly seedy meal at the only café in town. We discover the municipal campsite, which has a lone RV parked in some deep grass beside railroad tracks. No shelter, no tables, no toilets, no water. Back at the motel, which obviously is barely functioning, a sleepy-eyed teenager appears after several moments of knocking and asks if we have a reservation. Now I've heard everything! He scratches around and produces a couple of keys and the beds actually look usable – but only just.

Behind bent and cracked blinds on our picture window, orange streaks of cloud turn to deep red as the sun sinks beyond blunted cliffs curving around what looks like river valleys in the far distance. The east-to-west highway that meets our northbound mess of pot holes snakes into the sunset. Maybe we will have better roads tomorrow. A lilac bush is blooming in the dirt yard by the motel office.

We have left the Red Coat Trail to dip south, closer to the U.S. border, thereby avoiding busier towns and roads closer to the TransCanada Highway. However, the population is so sparse, I can't imagine anything being very busy anywhere in Saskatchewan. But I have heard a few horror stories of narrow roads with too much traffic to the north, and this southern route was recommended by my friend who "knows Saskatchewan like the back of his hand." It sounded intriguing at the time. Small towns, friendly people, rolling ranch land, the Big Muddy Badlands, easy cycling terrain.

One thing not mentioned was the clarity of light. We have come away from wheatlands flattened by unceasing wind, and I'm startled by hills rising to clear brown or black or green or sometimes blue, depending on the angle of the sun. After our overcast early morning, I watch as pure white clouds scurry along a brilliant blue sky to meet the horizon. The world is in sharp contrasts, much like we three musketeers. We have cycled into a little-visited part of Canada and definitely are an anomaly here.

Curiosity gets the better of one old codger driving a pickup. He stops on the road three times to chat with Granny M. He finally halts Grand Père who is bringing up the rear and asks how old she is. Grand Père tells him forty-seven. Granny M is speechless when he tells us this, then we all howl! He is off by more than a decade. Too young? Too old? Whatever the case, Mr. Curious slowly disappears behind us.

It feels like we are going to the moon again. We are skirting the Big Muddy Badlands. Clear skies, a little tailwind, many hills, range land as well as wheat fields, dusty towns with very few facilities. It's even difficult to buy groceries. About 3:00 p.m. we are still at least twenty-five kilometres from a hoped-for campsite (it's difficult to get accurate information from tourist centres or locals, as most know only their immediate vicinities, so we are hoping it's around twenty-five kilometres) when another curious rancher in a pickup pulls over ahead of me and waits. When I catch up he tells me that he passed us yesterday on his way north to a cattlemen's meeting regarding the mad cow disaster. "Where you all headin'?" When I tell him, he scowls and tells me it's further than twenty-five kilometres and we might not make it before dark as there's a gravel road entrance to the campground that he's not sure about. Could be another ten kilometres. Why don't we come to his place? We can camp in his yard. His name's Mike, and his wife Tammy does tours for visitors to the Big Muddy outlaw caves up behind his spread. They're used to unexpected company.

This rings a bell. A man at the tourist centre at Coronach where we stopped for lunch and supplies mentioned there was a rancher on our route who occasionally has space for campers. We should watch for the Circle Y Ranch. But I haven't planned on stopping at a ranch unannounced. Now, lucky us, here's the perfect invitation. The Circle Y is just a few bends up the road. A few bends plus a long hill.

From the top I glimpse an idyllic scene: red-roofed ranch home, several barns, horses, cows, machinery, all neatly nestled in a valley that I descend into all too quickly. I rattle over a cattle guard under an overhead sign-post for the Circle Y Ranch and follow Mike about a kilometre up to his house. This is as close to paradise as we are going to get for a long time; maybe ever.

I buy a copy of Mike's *Badland Bounty*, a collection of his cowboy poems illustrated by his artist wife Tammy. An old bunkhouse is her gallery and the backdrop for her talk on the famous outlaws of the Big Muddy. Some names are familiar! Bird feeders hung along the veranda of the bunkhouse attract American Golden Finches nonstop. We pitch our tents between the gallery and a small guest house with a toilet, sink, and a stove to cook on. I pass on using a fridge full of vials and syringes full of veterinary medicines; outside will be cool enough for the yogurt I bought for tomorrow's breakfast! Showers are up at the main house. When I ask if there's a cold beer around, it's passed along for free. They won't let us pay for camping either. Give something to your favourite charity, someone who needs it, Mike says.

The night is more than cool. I am warm enough but Grand Père says he is borderline. Granny M insists that she never gets cold. The hard part is the condensation on the tents. They are dripping in the morning, and we need an early start to beat the afternoon heat. Every day has been getting warmer, but wet tents make early packing up difficult. This problem will plague our camping for the rest of the trip. I could use my tarp as an extra fly over the tent, which may keep the tent dry, but finding support for the tarp in high winds and rain is difficult. Plus, I would still have a wet tarp to pack up. So I keep the tarp for emergencies only, usually for covering rough ground.

Badlands are left behind as more wheatland engulfs us. Moderate winds have come around to face us and progress is slow. Hills and more hills. This part of Saskatchewan is anything but flat! The southern route we follow has very few services, or even people for that matter. However, we manage to find real campgrounds – one is a large modern sports facility literally in the middle of nowhere – that usually have adequate shower facilities, but charge $15 per tent, even when we share the same site. When I complain, I'm told this is a government regulation. An RV or camper with six people pays the same per site fee as each of us, although there is an additional charge for hookups. But the basic fee doesn't change, and no proprietor will give us a break. This is not good news for Saskatchewan – $45 for three single tents is over the top.

At Estevan there's a library (that charges) for emails; a bike shop that gives us free cleanings and tuneups (but uses WD40 on the chains, I'm disappointed to learn after the deed has been done – this stuff collects more dirt than repels it) and charges Grand Père only $10 for a new tire. At Canadian Tire I buy a $25 tent with poles that match mine for length but not for tips; however, I can cut the tips to fit if necessary. I have split one of my poles at a connection with the shock cord and have managed to repair it with a splint and duct tape that is holding for the moment. With the new poles, I will have a spare if I need it, so I give the new tent minus its poles to the young man who assisted me in the store – he can't believe his good fortune as all he has to do is supply his own poles. There is a laundromat in town, a large grocery store for nutritious food – our first in a while – and all this fits into a day off. I need a day off to recover from my day off!

One thing about campgrounds is the noise. Some people try to be quiet, but a lot don't give a damn and there's no escape from loud voices, vehicles coming and going, music, even TVs, into the wee hours. But then, the Stanley Cup hockey playoffs are probably keeping most of Canada awake! However, sleep deprivation is becoming a recurring condition. Pedal on, Grandma, pedal on....

We are almost out of Saskatchewan, but not before a famous thunderstorm of the prairies hits. We have spitting rain off and on, and wind from the southeast while we head northeast.

Some hills, lonely cemeteries, wheat and more wheat. At Oxbow there's a campsite down a steep hill beside the Souris River. Granny M and Grand Père stop for a beer, but I need food and backtrack to a roadside hamburger stand just before the turnoff to the campsite. A woman approaches with the usual questions, but she is obviously a cyclist. How far have you come today? Where was the wind? How were the hills? Did you have rain? How far are you going tomorrow? She tells me there's a campground at Melita just over the Manitoba border that I can probably make. Then she adds rather wistfully, "I've done some touring, mostly down into the States and back, and would love to do what you're doing." I've heard this wishful thinking more than once over the last few days, and I am inspired – just keep pedalling, I tell myself.

I eat my hamburger while she buys her ice cream. Before leaving she tells me she lives just across the river from our campsite. "If you need anything, just give me a shout. My name is Gloria. Just watch that sky," she warns in parting.

The river is down one and a half kilometres of gravel road. Rain starts, then stops. I get my tent up. Grand Père has a split tent pole that he thinks he has time to repair. But the sky has other plans. Thunder closely followed by lightning splits the air a little down river. Instantly, huge black clouds roll over us, and just as I dive into my tent with my folding chair and sleeping bag, they open up.

My bike is totally exposed; I hope my panniers are closed.

Thank goodness I have my chair. I set it up and watch. Hail stones the size of nickels bounce off my tent and also up from the ground like popped corn. It feels like a pack of monkeys is in the trees over my head pelting my tent with small stones or maybe plum pits from their lunch. Do monkeys eat plums? These are novel ideas, just as this storm is a novel experience in a tent. I am not frightened as the thunder and lightning seem to be moving further down river, but I do wonder about the river flash flooding. I am only footsteps away from the riverbank, which is already full to the brim.

The downpour and hail storm don't last long. When I emerge, I find Grand Père and Granny M have managed to get our bikes under the shelter by the restrooms so I'm in fairly good shape, but Grand Père's tent is in pieces and soaked. Granny M has also erected her tent before sheltering from the storm with the bikes and Grand Père.

Gloria and her husband, Ken, drive over to see if we are okay. They offer to bring a tent to Grand Père, but after they leave, Grand Père shrugs at the whole scene and takes off for the motel up the hill. Granny M and I decide to stay put until Gloria and Ken return and advise that is not a good idea. They have checked the weather forecast and there is more heavy rain plus thunder and high winds on the way. And there have been a couple of twisters spotted just north of us. Listen to the locals, right?

We lock our bikes, grab some packs with clothes and toothbrush, and get chauffeured up the hill by Gloria and Ken who join us for dinner at the motel. After dinner, Ken returns with Maureen, the local campground supervisor, to move our bikes into a locked storage area next to the restrooms. "Better to not take any chances," they say. The night is punctuated with claps of thunder and pelting rain along with pinging hail. By morning the storm has moved on; there's even a little watery sunshine. Maureen delivers us back to the campsite where I am relieved to find my tent where I left it, as if nothing untoward has happened over the past sixteen hours. We unlock, dry out, and pack up. Next stop – Manitoba!

Is there a chance that in all the rest of our cycling trip we will have rescue stories to match those of Saskatchewan? Phil covers two provinces and will catch up via email at the end of the trip;

Ruthie and her van will eventually catch us back home in Canmore; Gloria and Ken will follow the rest of the ride via email updates, as will MaryLynne and Walt. Mike and Tammy will be remembered in photos and through their book. There has been so much hospitality offered and interest in our adventure that it's almost overwhelming. Still, I can't help but wonder who Mr.Curious is, or where he is now.

For now, it's two thumbs up! The sun is shining and the wind's behind us! We've covered 716 Saskatchewan kilometres over eight days of riding over pot-holed roads, chasing lilacs, serenaded by an infinite variety of song birds, hanging on in the wind. A true Canadian prairie experience!

Logistics

Our southern route almost scrapes the U.S. border, and it is anything but flat! Potent prairie winds live up to their reputation, okay when they are pushing us, but bike-stopping when we are against them. They are as unpredictable as the clouds and rain that follow them – one day is wind with no rain, another is rain with little wind. When we need rescuing from the elements, angels appear. The curious get curiouser and curiouser.

May 30, Sunday   (day 30).

Ride: Eastend to Ponteix (motel).
Follow the Red Coat Trail, Route 13 east. Ponteix beginning of French Saskatchewan with huge church, murals, grain elevators. Another semi-ghost town. Very little traffic; very few people.

Facilities: Lunch at Shaunavon, also groceries and camping at municipal park. No other services en route. Motel, restaurant, groceries at Ponteix. Campsite near motel.

Total distance: 116 km.
Average speed: 19 kph.
Maximum speed: 50 kph.

Monday, May 31   (day 31).

Ride: Ponteix to Gravelbourg (B&B).
Follow Route 13 east to Route 58 north. (Hitchhiked to escape wind last 20 km.) Gravelbourg is famous for its cathedral with painted walls and imported stained glass windows.

Facilities: Lunch at Kincaid, Lafleche. Heritage House B&B, restaurants, bank, T.I., groceries in Gravelbourg.

Total distance: 72 km (plus 20 km by car).
Average speed: 21 kph.
Maximum speed: 39 kph.

Alternative camping:
Thomson Lake campground on Route 58 approximately 5 km north of Lafleche (minimal services) and 15 km south of Gravelbourg.

Tuesday, June 1   (day 32).

Ride: Gravelbourg to Rockglen (motel).
Follow Route 43 east to Route 2 south to Route 18 east. Long stretches of nothing. Sections of road in major disrepair – but scenery magnificent with many deep coulees and steep hills through wheat fields as well as cattle ranges that skirt the Big Muddy Badlands.

Facilities: Restaurants, groceries, bank, T.I. in Assiniboia. Motel, café in Rockglen. Town campsite has no water or toilet facilities.

Total distance: 123 km.
Average speed: 20 kph.

Alternative camping:
St. Victor's Petroglyphs Provincial Park camping or camping at Willow Bunch on Route 36 going south, instead of Route 2. Route 2 in major disrepair. Rockglen offers little for facilities or groceries. Shop in Assiniboia on the way.

Wednesday, June 2   (day 33).

Ride: Rockglen to Circle Y Ranch.
Follow Route 18 east. Circle Y recommended at T. I. in Coronach who could phone for permission plus directions. We followed owner who offered his campsite when encountering us on the road. Route 18 is hilly, has little traffic, is in fairly good condition. Ranch is about 20 km east of Big Beaver at about 600 metres elevation.

Facilities: Groceries, café at Coronach. Shower, toilet, water at Circle Y Ranch.

Total distance: 93 km.

Alternative Camping:
Clear Lake Regional Campground approximately another 30 km east of Burgess's Circle Y Ranch.

Thursday, June 3   (day 34).

Ride: Circle Y Ranch to Oungre Regional Recreation Centre and Campground.
Follow Route 18 east before turning north on Hwy 35 for 2 km to campsite. Route is hilly through rolling wheat lands.

Facilities: Only food en route is café at Lake Alma. Camping at Oungre Regional Recreation Centre & Campground. $15 each tent. Showers available, food at local restaurant and centre's snack bar; no groceries available in area.

Total distance: 96 km.
Average speed: 16 kph.
Maximum speed: 35 kph.

Friday, June 4   (day 35).

Ride: Oungre Recreation Centre to Estevan.
Follow Route 18 east on flat road. Need lots of water.

Facilities: No food en route. All services in Estevan including library, groceries, Wal-Mart and Canadian Tire. Hidden Valley Campground 3 km from town; $15 per tent.

Joe's Bike Shop in Estevan.

Total distance: 63 km.

Saturday, June 5   (day 36).

Rest day.

Sunday, June 6   (day 37).

Ride: Estevan to Oxbow.
Follow Route 18 east (motel). Flat ride!

Facilities: Food stop at Bienfait. Camping at Bow Valley

Campground on Souris River at Oxbow. Groceries, motel, restaurants in town.

Total distance: 71 km.
Average speed: 13 kph.
Maximum speed: 38 kph.

Alternative Camping: Municipal campground at Carievale about 40 km east of Oxbow.

Monday, June 7   (day 38).

Ride: Oxbow to Melita, Manitoba.
Follow Route 18 (Saskatchewan) east to Route 3 (Manitoba), the Red Coat Trail. Mostly flat, a few low hills.

Facilities: Lunch in Pierson, MB. Camping at Melita municipal campground, no charge. Groceries in Melita.

Total distance: 100 km.
Average speed: 27 kph.
Maximum speed: 41 kph.

Manitoba

License plate motto: Friendly Manitoba
Official flower: prairie crocus
Official bird: great grey owl

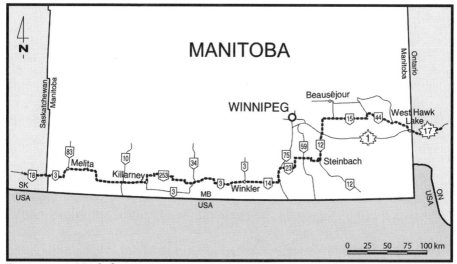

Route across Manitoba

*The wheat in spring was like a giants' bolt of silk
Unrolled over the earth.*
~ The Wind our Enemy by Anne Marriott,
1913-1997

Highlights

I am inside the wind. The push from behind is equal to the wind in my face, and clicking along at thirty on my cyclometre, I am suspended in a cocoon, enveloped in warm, still air. I want to shed my jacket, but know it's still cool on the outside. Being inside is similar to running before the wind in a sailboat. You don't feel air movement, yet you are leaving a wake behind. It's a surreal feeling, like pedalling in slow motion while my bike swallows pavement lined with fields of wheat.

I expect to land in the ditch when I turn off the wind and feel the extreme lean of my bike. It's difficult to believe that holding on will keep me moving forward because it's almost instinctive to just let go, or try for a controlled fall. Is this extreme biking? One good thing – I can sing all I want. No one hears my off-tune renditions of the silly nursery rhymes that mysteriously surface in my head. "This old man, he plays one, he plays nick-nack on my drum." "A-tisket, a-tasket, a green and yellow basket." Ella Fitzgerald's rendition has rhythm. It helps. I'm not carrying a Walkman for musical diversion, and the deafening wind can be soul-destroying.

A low pressure system loaded with wet weather plagues us, as well as the rest of Manitoba. There is little variation on the theme. Intermittent rain, wind in our face or at our back, sometimes on our side. The road surface changes dramatically at the border; no more pot holes, plus there are gravel shoulders. We are forced to cycle out in the road, which is good because now we are highly visible to the scant traffic, especially the extra-wide farm machinery passing us. The terrain is flat – very flat! And the colour is green when it isn't drowning in standing water in the fields. Crops are not getting planted; rivers are flooding.

We camp at Melita, but resort to a motel at Killarney where the night temperature is close to freezing. Killarney belies its Irish heritage except for the lake at its feet. The campgrounds are not inviting, nor is the town known as "The Wheat Capital of Southern Manitoba." We bypass the murals at Boissevain in a north headwind and don't even contemplate going south to the International Peace Gardens in the rain. Cold nights, along with the rain, are depressing. However, lilacs still bloom along the way.

A grocery stop at Pilot Mound spurs us on to La Rivière where a friendly-looking campground basks in rare evening sun. Alas, the campground has been vandalized on the weekend and the broken toilets and pulled-down showers are unusable. We retreat to an A frame cabin at Holiday Mountain Ski Resort and Golf Course, which has to be one of the smallest ski areas in Canada (two very short chair lifts, one T bar, one rope tow) along with one of the most vertical golf courses in North America. Cost? $30 a day to ski; $12 for a round of golf. A Manitoba bargain! I will return someday, I tell myself.

This is the day before my sixty-sixth birthday and I'm supposed to be about sixty kilometres further for a motel treat that is a gift from friends at home. The time-frame is according to the tentative schedule I compiled for my itinerary before beginning the trip. Considering the weather, I'm happy to be only sixty kilometres behind schedule, and the motel in Winkler is holding my room for me after I phone. The lady managing the cabin/ski/golf resort buys me a glass of birthday wine when I escape my disgruntled partners for an evening stroll around the grounds. It cheers me, but I suspect a mutiny is brewing. Grand Père has been suggesting that we should consider changing our route to possibly avoid some of Manitoba's nasty weather. From Winkler, the usual bike route skirts the south end of Lake of the Woods into Minnesota, U.S.A. for approximately seventy-five kilometres before rejoining Canada at Rainy River, Ontario. This route saves about two days cycling time, but it misses one of the most beautiful areas of Canada North that we will pedal through. I'm anxious to get to Kenora on the north end of the lake and then on to a real taste of wilderness cycling, all the while establishing my goal of creating a cross-Canada route that does not dip into the States. I keep reminding myself of my objectives. Another glass of wine dulls the rumblings back at the cabin.

Winkler is a quick sprint for sixty-four kilometres the next morning, and I get to the motel just ahead of the daily rain showers. Before

Grand Père and Granny M stop for lunch along the way, we agree to meet at the motel in Winkler later for dinner. They will camp at the municipal park a couple blocks from the motel. They wished me a happy birthday before departing, rather grudgingly perhaps?

The motel has a spa pool, whirlpool, and steam room. I could stay immersed for a week, but I'm distracted by emails at the library, then buying bike cleaning stuff as there's no bike shop in Winkler. After all the rain, my bike is a mess. I can at least clean the chain with some Varsol and a cheap toothbrush. I get a load of clothes into the motel laundry, then just as I turn on the steam room the fellow from the front desk appears with a portable phone. It's my husband back home along with my friends who have given me this wonderful birthday escape. They have also arranged for a newspaper interview at Steinbach the next day as well as an overnight stay with their relatives at a camping village just north of Steinbach which is over 100 kilometres from Winkler, most likely in strong winds and probably rain! We end our phone conversation with another arrangement – a truck pickup if we don't make it. "Here's the number, just in case."

The steam timer clicks off and I have no time for a rewind. There's my dirty bike waiting and it's already late in the afternoon. Maybe later....

My cycling partners do not show up for dinner, and I have been too busy to check on their campsite to see what's up. Dinner is a quiet time by myself, without a glass of wine in this dry Mennonite town – a sober celebration! But I am grateful for my first moments of solitude during the whole trip. The realization dawns that I'm actually doing what I've been focused on for several months now, and that my birthday is a milestone to mark my progress. There isn't even anyone to argue with about it.

When no one shows up for breakfast, I pack my bike and leave it in front of the motel as a sign that I'm around, and then walk to search for the campsite and two lost cyclists. They are fifteen minutes away and busy drying their tents when I arrive. There is an immediate if not hesitant conversation concerning the route ahead. Grand Père does not want to go north of the lake; Granny M also thinks we should go south through the U.S.. I listen to their arguments about weather delays and getting behind our tentative

Miniature horses — not seeing eye to eye!

schedule. I point out that the schedule was not written in stone, and certainly not something we are bound to follow, no matter what, especially with all the unknowns of the trip. Besides, we are off schedule by only one day, and almost into Ontario. Another ten days and we will be halfway. That's better timing than I had hoped for by this point in our odyssey.

Grand Père is obstinate. Granny M is upset. This is not going to be easy. I find a dry spot to sit while they continue to pack. After a few moments I tell them, "I'm not going south. If you guys want to go, that's fine. But I came on this trip to establish a bike route across Canada and I'm not giving up on my agenda."

Granny M is very angry! However, neither Grand Père or myself are really surprised at this turn of events. The split has been brewing for days and is reminiscent of Grand Père's repeated detours from the established routes of our U.S. trip. Also, I suspect he wants to be freed from accompanying two women through the Canadian wilderness on his bike, although at this point I don't know if he will continue with one or no female partner.

I tell Granny M where my bike and I will be waiting if she decides to join me. If she hasn't arrived within an hour, I will carry on by myself. I'm shaking as I walk away. Have I made the correct decision? Will I really be by myself, and will I really bike the wilderness alone? By the time I get to the motel, I feel surprisingly calm. Somewhere deep down, I know that I can do this, and I will give my best shot to actually accomplish what I have set out to do. Perhaps my biggest mistake has been to not go alone from the very beginning, but I've been through more than a few hellish moments thus far, and have gained more confidence as I've clicked off the distances. So, "Go for it, girl!" as my friend back home said to me yesterday on the phone. Her cheer is ringing in my ears!

I loiter in the motel lobby, wondering. I'm very aware of Granny M's attachment to Grand Père and that if she leaves him, it will be a big wrench. She will be forced to assume more responsibility for her bike as well as herself, as I have clearly stated from the beginning that this is an independent bike ride for everyone concerned. I am not here to be a leader or caregiver or bike mechanic. If someone wants to ride with me, they are responsible for both themselves and their equipment. The fact that Grand Père has taken Granny M under his wing has been his – and her – option.

When I planned the route, I communicated with both Granny M and Grand Père regarding their input. Granny M clearly stated she did not have any preferences and, as her knowledge of Canada was limited, she would agree with whatever I decided. I reviewed my route with her husband before we left so he would be familiar with my choices. Grand Père offered valuable input regarding our route in Québec; he also agreed to the northern routing around the lake. But he has changed his mind, and Granny M has to sever her umbilical cord to him if she comes with me. This is a threshold moment!

After a half-hour, she pedals up on the highway, but not along the back road from the campsite. I'm relieved she is here. However, I'm not looking forward to dealing with her anger. I know she is really pissed with me! And did she almost get lost already?

We are silent as we move out into a horrendous headwind, heading east and then north. Grand Père has to come this way also – for a while – but he is nowhere to be seen. Hopefully, we will meet again in Montréal. The two grannies are on our own!

The ride to Steinbach is almost my undoing. I clock a total of 104 kilometres before I bonk. I know I cannot go further. I have zigzagged north and east to get this far and every time I turn east, the wind whips me. The road surface on Route 75 going north to Winnipeg is almost as bad as that horrific pot-holed north/south spurt we had in Saskatchewan; perhaps it's worse. And then there's the wind. At St-Pierre-Jolys we are still thirty kilometres from Steinbach according to the map, with twenty-one kilometres going into the wind. It's 5:00 p.m. and we were supposed to meet the newspaper around 3:00. I phone the "just in case number" and within thirty minutes our ride arrives. We load our bikes into his pickup, and get to Steinbach for the newspaper interview at 6:00. Finally, we get delivered to the camping cabin another twenty kilometres north of Steinbach where our friends, Bennie and Myrna, are waiting with burgers on the barbecue and a bottle of champagne! There hasn't been time for Steinbach's Mennonite Heritage Centre which I was hoping to see.

After I shower and fall into bed, I look back on this traumatic day. While I was phoning in St-Pierre-Jolys, Granny M received an invitation to dinner at a man's house who wanted us to talk to his kids about our ride. We could have stopped if we had no appointments to keep, but I don't know if I would have been very enthusiastic about discussing my ride. Today's "hitting a wall" (in athlete's jargon) was a first for me, and I know I have not had enough rest time. Winkler was a half-day off chock full of work and emotionally draining decisions. The next short day will be at Kenora, which is a couple of days away. One thing for sure – if I don't keep pedalling, I won't ever get to Newfoundland.

"Sleep does wonders," Manitoba farmer

Sleep does wonders – along with a good breakfast. We head north an extra twenty kilometres to follow minor roads into Ontario and thereby avoid the TransCanada Highway. The Manitoba Cycling Association has issued a brochure regarding cycling in Manitoba and recommends alternate routes to the TransCanada: "Of all the highway related cycling accidents and deaths, virtually all of them occur on this highway." They also advise against taking Route 75 which grabbed us yesterday for twenty kilometres of tailwind rather than turn south even for six kilometres into the headwind before turning east. It was nice being pushed by the wind, but between truck traffic and its appalling surface, Route 75 is definitely unsafe. Today we will do as advised by other cyclists. The wind has dropped, and it's not raining for a change.

Before we leave the campground, Granny M skids in loose gravel, falls, and snaps the repair clamp holding her rear pannier onto her rack where her braze-on should be. It's the original $5 repair from Hope, B.C. which has been reinforced a couple of times, but which has held until now. We need something like a strong piece of wire to hold the rack in place; our twist ties don't do it. We get twenty-one kilometres up the road before they break completely and send us scouting for a piece of roadside trash with some wire. When three young men towing a small fishing boat pull over at the intersection where we have stopped to turn east, we approach them for maybe a C-clamp in their toolbox? Sure enough, they have two that fit and manage to get them in place on the rack. These clamps hold for the rest of the trip. Granny M is most grateful, and so am I! This must be a good omen.

Our last night in Manitoba is a campground at Brereton Lakes, eight kilometres north of our secondary road. We find some groceries before pedalling up to the lakes where we are greeted by swarms of mosquitoes and non-potable water. The park has hauled in a large tank of drinking water so we can fill our bottles and hydration packs, but cooking and cleanup is minimal and there are no showers. We pay $10 for this lack of service! At bedtime, barricaded in my tent behind bug screens, I write in my journal that I feel like I have finally hit my stride today – strange! Is this because Grand Père has gone south and I am free to pursue my own directions? Granny M appears to be putting her anger behind her

– and me. Hitting my wall seems a long time ago.

Our last day in Manitoba takes us into Canadian Shield hills covered with boreal forest. We stop at West Hawk Lake, a meteor crater several kilometres wide filled with water 115 metres deep. The hole is almost over-flowing; a fuel dock is barely floating. I'm happy to leave rainy, wet, windy Manitoba behind, but not happy to join the TransCanada Highway to do so. What a blast of trucks! At least there is a wide shoulder and a big sign – "Welcome to Ontario, More to Discover". Yes, we're coming!

Manitoba has been 628 kilometres over six days to Kenora, Ontario.

Logistics

We finally hit flat prairies. Rain and wind do not let up for most of the six days we pedal across the southern edge of the province. Fields are flooded; rivers are over-flowing. We follow the Red Coat Trail until we cut northeast of Winnipeg and head east to Lake of the Woods, Ontario, managing to avoid the TransCanada Highway until we reach the Ontario border. Canada's multi-ethnic heritage is evident in the French, Irish, German, Indian, and English names of towns we pass through. And of course there's the Mennonite stronghold south and east of Winnipeg. My tourist brochure tells me that the word Manitoba is from the Ojibway word Manitou, meaning spirit. I feel that spirit – in the wind as well as with the friendly people in all the small towns along the way – and will always remember Manitoba for it. Roads in Manitoba have gravel shoulders. Beware!

Tuesday, June 8   (day 39).

Ride: Melita to Killarney (motel).
Follow Route 3 east. Flat ride. Lots of water, rivers over-flowing.

Facilities: No services en route. Take food from Melita. Boissevain murals north on Route 10; Turtle Mountain Provincial Park and International Peace Gardens south on Route 10. Motels, restaurants, bank, groceries in Killarney.

Total distance: 110 km.
Average speed: 20 kph.
Maximum speed: 36 kph.

Alternative Camping: Killarney Agricultural Society Campground near lake; Boissevain; Turtle Mountain Provincial Park

Wednesday, June 9 (day 40).

Ride: Killarney to La Rivière (motel).
Follow Route 3 east. We took "short cut" on Route 253, a hilly road through the Pembina River Valley from Killarney to Pilot Mound. To avoid extra hills, stay on Route 3.

Facilities: Few facilities en route; take snacks from Killarney. Food and groceries in Pilot Mound. Overnight at Holiday Mountain Ski and Golf Resort a few kilometres before La Rivière.

Total distance: 94 km.
Average speed: 16 kph.
Maximum speed: 45 kph.

Alternative Camping: Pembina Valley Centennial Park on Pembina River at La Rivière.

Thursday, June 10 (day 41)

Ride: La Rivière to Winkler (motel and camping).
Follow Route 3 east. Flat riding.

Facilities: Lunch, library in Morden. Overnight in Winkler at Heartland Motel on Route 3. Shopping, library, groceries, restaurants, bank, library, camping in Winkler.

Total distance: 64 km.

Alternative Camping: Winkler Tourist Park.

Friday, June 11 (day 42).

Ride: Winkler to Steinbach (friend's camper).
Follow Routes 3/14 east to 75 south for 6 km to 201 east to 218 north to 59 north to 205 east to 12 north to Steinbach. This is a zigzag route around Winnipeg, approximately 120 km Winkler to Steinbach. I pedalled Route 3/14 east to 75 north to 23 east to 200 north to 205 east to St-Pierre-Jolys, 104 km, then hitchhiked 25 km to Steinbach and on to Ste. Anne and the Lilac Resort to stay at friend's camper. Route 75 is not safe for cycling; use as little as possible as connector to eastbound roads. Mennonite Heritage Centre in Steinback; historic churches at Sarto on Route 205.

Facilities: Lunch at Morris on Route 75, St. Malo on Route 218, St-Pierre-Jolys on Route 59. All facilites (except liquor) in Steinbach

Total distance: 104 km (+ 25 km by car).

Saturday, June 12   (day 43).

Ride: Ste. Anne (Lilac Resort) to Rennie and Brereton Lake Campground.
Follow Route 12 north to 15 east to 11 north to 44 east. From Lilac Resort, Ste. Anne to Brereton Lake is 125 km (from Steinbach add another 20 km). Brereton Lake is 8 km north on Route 307 off Route 44. Mostly flat riding; hills beginning near Brereton Lakes.

Facilities: Lunch stop on Elma on popular bike route. Groceries in Rennie. Camping at Brereton Lake Campground in Whiteshell Provincial Park; $10 per tent. Non-potable water at campground (in 2004); no showers.

Total distance: 125 km.
Average speed: 21 kph.
Maximum speed: 33 kph.

Sunday, June 13   (day 44).

Ride: Brereton Lake to Kenora, Ontario (motel).
Follow Route 44 east to West Hawk Lake and TransCanada Highway 1 & 17 (in Ontario). T.C.H. is bombardment of heavy traffic and trucks; also wide shoulder with rough pavement and potholes and trash. Watch for broken glass. Ride gets hilly close to Kenora. Kenora known for murals and museum.

Facilities: Lunch at West Hawk Lake on Ontario border; gas station at Clearwater Bay; nothing else until Kenora – long stretch with many hills. Motels, restaurants, shopping, post office, bank, library ($2 per hour for Internet), bike shop in Kenora.

Total distance: 94 km.
Average speed: 20 kph.
Maximum speed: 48 kph.

Alternative Camping: Rushing River Provincial Park located on Rushing River a few kilometres south of intersection of Routes 17A, 17, and 71 just east of downtown Kenora.

Ontario

License plate motto: Yours to Discover
Official flower: white trillium
Official bird: common loon

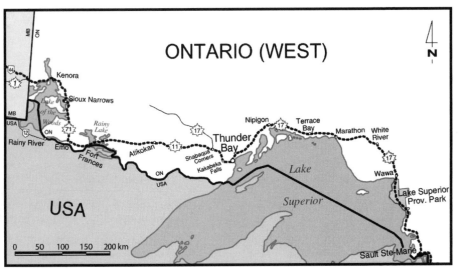

Route across Ontario (West)

"I've always wanted to do what you two are doing."
~ Jack Layton to the Cycling Grannies
Thunder Bay, ON, July, 2004

*"We had commenced our great adventure....
We were at times very serious and concerned....
Above all, we loved this country and loved exploring
and painting it."*

~ Lawren Harris, 1885-1970

Route across Ontario (East)

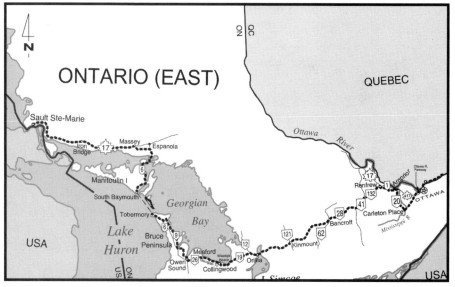

Highlights

My proposed itinerary breaks Ontario into western Ontario followed by Manitoulin Island, the Bruce Peninsula and Canadian Shield country to Ottawa and the Québec border. Ontario's total distance is almost twice that of British Columbia, yet I hope to cover this mid-quarter of Canada in the same number of days it took to straddle all those mountains in the west. I now face long stretches of isolated wilderness that look intimidating on the map. Their challenge makes me itch to get going, denying my body's fatigue. I am forced to linger in Kenora for emails, to visit a bike shop for general maintenance, and mailing used maps and other tidbits home – enough work to fill a half-day off, but still leaving a little down time to fortify me for the next surge.

Kenora, situated all by itself on the north shore of Lake of the Woods, is known as the Muskie fishing capital of the world. This is fishing paradise. To prove it, a giant muskie sculpture rises from the waterfront park that skirts downtown and the public library ($2 per hour for Internet use), and restaurants feature fresh lake fish on their menus. We learn that although we are the first cross-country cyclists to pass through the bike shop this season, we will not be the last. We are in cycling territory, and I am encouraged. I'm not the only cyclist aspiring to follow my northern route!

As we enter town dodging rain showers, Granny M's rear tire gets punctured by a wire sliver shed from a shredded truck tire (every cyclist's nemesis along truck routes). We repair the damage while sheltering in an industrial building's restroom. It is unlocked for us by a man hoping for business at his water-logged hotdog stand parked in front of the building. A friendly introduction to Ontario!

Kenora is also famous for its murals. I photograph one depicting the town's historic change from its original name of Rat Portage, located in Manitoba before the "Rat Portage Wars" in 1883 moved boundaries and placed re-named Kenora in Ontario. The new name and new boundaries have always been contentious. Being governed by industrialized far-distant Toronto, which can't begin

Kenora mural, Ontario

to understand the needs of this land of fishermen, loggers, and First Nations people who service the fishing industry their lives depend upon, does not make sense to the locals, either in 1883 or today. Their pleas for more money for services, especially road maintenance, routinely fall on deaf ears.

We follow the city route of the TransCanada Highway (there is a bypass around Kenora) to leave civilization behind. Rivers and creeks are overflowing their banks. A few kilometres out of Kenora, the TransCanada splits, #17 going east to Dryden, the main truck route and one of the most notoriously dangerous sections across Canada, and #71 going south along the lake, still used by truckers but less so than the Dryden route. My replacement tent poles (ordered via my husband back home) have been rerouted to a friend near Ottawa as they didn't get sent in time to catch me in Kenora at the home of another friend-of-a-friend. My duct tape and splint repair is still holding, and I have the ill-fitting spares just in case.

We pedal south over gentle hills skirting the lake shore on recently resurfaced two-lane road with narrow shoulders. There is minimal truck traffic. The ride from Kenora to Sioux Narrows rivals the Cowboy Trail in Alberta for beauty and wilderness, but here it is more wild. There is no open range land with shy pronghorns or bushy-tailed foxes watching from a distance. Instead boreal forests, hills, and mini-lakes capped with rock outcrops crowned with more trees hug the road. I'm on the lookout for moose and bear. I spy what looks like a giant white-tailed deer – it must be four metres tall – flashing its tail through the trees; turkey vultures circle overhead. I come over a slight rise and almost collide with a black bear that is every bit as big as me and my bike. It's just about to cross the road in front of me, and my first thought is that it could get hit by a car. Then I realize it is in danger of being hit by me! I brake suddenly and startle both of us. It turns on a dime and is off into the woods. I stop to take a deep breath and watch it disappear. By the time Granny M comes up from behind, it's gone. A little further on a huge tortoise waddles across the road. What next?

This is actually a day without rain! And no wind! Clouds hover, clearing in the evening and leaving enough streaks for a wispy yellow-orange sunset. An attendant at the provincial park gives us the unexpected news that we are still several kilometres from Sioux Narrows for groceries, after which we would have to backtrack to camp. It's already 6:00 p.m.. Maybe we should try the RV fishing camp we've just passed – they have a camp store. We go back, wind our way up a steep entrance road and drop into an idyllic camp on an inlet of Lake of the Woods. The store stocks snack food only. It looks like chips, juice, and cookies for supper, until the fellows next door invite us for a beer and to talk about our trip. They are Americans who have been coming here for years to fish. They stay in the same dilapidated hundred-year-old cabin for its atmosphere, at least two families (I lose count) sleeping wherever, smoking, playing cards, drinking beer, and fishing. The women don't interrupt their card game or chain of cigarettes when we appear, but offer fresh rolls "made from scratch" by one of the men, slathered with real butter. We grannies make a considerable dent in the pan of still-warm rolls, down a couple of beers, chat with the men about our adventures. We do not get invited for dinner, which looks like it will be too late for us anyway. We finish the chips and retire to our showers and tents. While I munch a couple of oatmeal cookies for dessert, I watch the sunset fade into soft tints over the water. Loons echo their evening calls, over and over. I note in my journal that I would not have missed this part of Canada for anything!

Sunset, Lake of the Woods

Two months from today we will fly home. It's June 15; at day forty-six we are almost halfway along my projected ninety-eight days of pedalling. We still have Lake Superior to put behind us so we won't be halfway in distance for another 800 kilometres; however, we are still just one day behind our tentative schedule, and it's still cool and wet. Locals are waiting for their summer that isn't happening. Lilacs are in full bloom in Kenora and Fort Francis, a month behind their usual time. Early mornings leave frost on car windshields.

There are trees and more trees – a little less water on land but more from the sky. Rain drives us to motels. Granny M's bike tuneup in Kenora doesn't hold and she pedals with a rear derailleur that won't shift into higher gears until the next bike shop in Fort Frances where a technician named Chris discovers a badly frayed cable that has been tuned too tightly, causing the shifter to jam. She also has a chain and gears chock-full of clumps of grit that were supposed to have been cleaned out in Kenora. My chain is also still full of grit. We are told to ask specifically for a "drive-train clean" next time. A bike mechanic I am not – but I'm learning a lot about maintenance.

Our average speed hovers around twenty kilometres per hour, which is a good omen, especially as the TransCanada Highway

#11 between Fort Frances and Thunder Bay is being resurfaced, leaving stretches of the old road that show extreme decay. Despite bike shop delays and the rain, we still make good progress while dodging construction zones. Just before Kakabeka Falls we arrive at an outfitter's camp that a woman at the store of the derelict motel and campsite where we were planning to stop secured for us by phone. She knew there was no other place either to camp or motel as campsites are in poor condition or non-existent and motels are fully occupied with work crews – geologists surveying or prospecting for minerals, road construction crews, miners employed short-term, or specialists cleaning up defunct mines. We have found that once a crew's 6:00 a.m. breakfast is finished, roadside restaurants at motels close until dinner time. So obtaining food and sometimes accommodation has been a challenge.

A good tail wind helps us pedal on for a total of 141 kilometres to the outfitter's camp – our longest day yet. We cross the north/south Continental Divide to learn all waters flowing north of this point will end in the Arctic Ocean and all waters flowing south drain in the Atlantic. So we've now crossed the north/south divide as well as the east/west (at the Alberta/B.C. border). I am impressed! This is still Canada North but getting closer to Canada East.

We arrive at 5:45 for dinner at 6:00. "Don't be late – it's moose steak tonight." The marinated and oven-braised steak is not very different in taste from a tough beef steak treated the same way, and it is cooked to perfection! I have been feeling cheated as no moose have appeared on the road since the loner in Cypress Hills; now I at least get to taste the meat. Our final surprise for the day is learning from our dinner partners, a four-man crew decommissioning a nickel mine nearby, that Grand Père has stayed with them two nights ago. No doubt he is pedalling hard!

Kakabeka Falls – it has a ring to it that Longfellow must have heard. In this land of the Ojibway the Indian maiden, Green Mantle called to Hiawatha near these majestic falls – known as the Niagara of the North – where as many as 2,000 trappers gathered to trade their furs with the North West Trading Company in the early 1800s. Pictorials along the trail to the falls recount Indian legends as well as explorations of the Northwest Passage in this fur trading

Kakabeka Falls

empire of the New World. We follow in traders' footsteps taking photographs. Is that Green Mantle I hear above the rush of water? When we emerge in the parking lot, it is filled with about fifty Harley-Davidsons and their riders. The contrast is too much. I can only laugh. But still ringing in the tumble of the falls is the "Song of Hiawatha," a foretaste of Longfellow's other immortal story of Evangeline in the land of Acadia in an eastern Canada yet to be discovered by two cycling grannies from the west. Longfellow got around, especially for someone who never set foot in Canada! All his writings were composed from researching writings and descriptions made by others. However he wrote them, they will no doubt be remembered in many imaginations similar to my own, over many more years and in many lands.

Thirty kilometres from the falls, we are in the outskirts of Thunder Bay. The road surface is so bad and construction hauling trucks are so determined to run me into the raised curb (a poor excuse for a shoulder) that I duck into the nearest Robin's Doughnuts to escape. I am shaken from a couple of very near misses. After the restroom, I regroup and order a bowl of soup. The staff has seen our bikes and of course the questions start: Where have you come from? Where are you going? How long have you been on the road? How many kilometres a day do you do? Everyone is curious. While the third degree is progressing, several large black cars pull in and several people in black suits come in for coffee. This is a strange retinue. I can't resist asking one woman in a black suit what the occasion is – maybe a state funeral or something? "No," she replies. "I'm a RCMP officer and I've just come off a six hour flight to join Jack Layton's campaign here in Thunder Bay. We try to accompany the candidates on their tours. I just came from Paul Martin's camp." Obviously, she's showing me her nonpartisan position, but she is also tired from traipsing after election campaigners. It's about ten days before the federal election for prime minister and things are in high gear. Luckily, I have been able to watch the candidates' debates at our motels in the rain, so I know who the principals are, but am still surprised when Jack Layton, the NDP candidate, appears for his own cup of coffee. And of course he has stopped to meet the locals. What he didn't expect to run into was two grannies cycling across Canada.

"I've always wanted to do what you're doing!" his eyes sparkle over his coffee cup. "I don't own a car, just seven bikes hanging in my garage. My wife and I usually tour on a tandem." He is more than enthused. He is positively impressed and wants to come with us! I tell him every candidate should cycle across Canada. "Go – and take Paul with you! You'll see what the roads are really like." The suggestion that he should take Paul (as in Paul Martin, the incumbent Liberal contender) along brings a hearty chuckle. We banter back and forth and he tells me about his plans for cycle paths in Toronto. "It's so cheap to do! But I want to know where you are going." All the way, we tell him, including across Newfoundland.

"You must get to the Iles de la Madeleine if at all possible. The best seafood is at a little shack on the very end of the top island." It's on our itinerary, I tell him. "And PEI's Confederation Trail is a must. Let me see your bikes!" His staff offer to take our photos with Jack and our bikes; just as we're posing for our own cameras, a photojournalist for the Thunder Bay Chronicle Journal arrives and snaps a classic grass-roots shot which appears on the front page of the paper the next morning.

It's Sunday and the newspaper is distributed free of charge to our motel room. When I open the door to retrieve a muffin breakfast from the lobby, there I am, a cycling grannie going across Canada, staring up from the floor along with a grinning Jack Layton and my cycling partner from Canmore, Alberta. This is a huge joke – and it's real! Layton is my candidate of choice, but not my partner's, so it's a good thing he doesn't have his arms around us in the newspaper shot. Especially as we are now readily identified as "The Cycling Grannies." The whole incident makes me chuckle the rest of the ride. Thanks, Jack. Fingers crossed for the election!

We try and find a constituency office to obtain absentee ballots so we can vote, but are not successful. I am disappointed. I want my vote to count for the candidate who doesn't own a car!

There's an email from Grand Père from Sudbury. He says the road surface gets better after Nipigon, about 100 kilometres from Thunder Bay. He is on his way to Montréal via the northern route; we are going south across Manitoulin Island. He asks us to contact him when we get closer to Montréal. Susan, who pedalled with Grand Père and myself across the U.S. last year, and her husband John are coming to Montréal from Brooklyn, New York to pedal with us in Québec. Hooray! It will be a real pleasure to ride with Sue again. She is an experienced cyclist who is genuinely nice to everyone she comes in contact with – a rarity in cycle touring, which often produces anxiety and stress and fatigue with sometimes nasty consequences. Québec will be a lot of fun, but first I have to get across Ontario.

There are so many stories....one of my favourites is my rescue at Nipigon by Mike, a recreation cyclist who would rather operate a bike shop than work nightshift at the sawmill. But at the moment he is only building bikes for a hobby and incidently offering assistance to other local cyclists in his basement where he has accumulated minimal equipment. It's late morning when I pedal into the outskirts of Nipigon, and I know there's something seriously wrong with my bike. I can't shift it properly. When I stop at the Tourist Information Centre to inquire about bike shops in the area, I'm directed to Lavina, who knows everyone in town and figures Mike is my only hope. She phones and learns he has been asleep after working all night, but he will try and help if she brings me to his house. She leads in her car while I attempt more shifting to test and make sure that I really do need a bike mechanic. There's no doubt – I'm not going to make this machine work properly without assistance.

I've had a professional service at the bike shop in Thunder Bay two days ago. The road has been rough and I've had a minor fall, but that doesn't explain this new development. Mike adjusts, I test ride, and we adjust some more. Finally, a close inspection of the front derailleur reveals stripped screws in its attachment to the frame. The derailleur is not holding in position, and there is no choice but to repair and possibly replace the derailleur, a task out of Mike's league. I am 100 kilometres from the bike shop in Thunder Bay. Mike worked last night and has had only a couple hours of sleep, but offers to take me to Thunder Bay in his visiting father-in-law's van. He wants to take his bike also, so this is good timing - the van, his bike, my derailed derailleur. He phones to make sure our parts are available, and off we go.

Rain falls in torrents on the drive. It's almost impossible to keep moving in the van, let alone on a bike. We would have been sheltering for this one, but places to stop are few and far between. More good timing!

Keith at the bike shop takes things in hand. Two hours later I have a new derailleur (the screws were previously stripped and re-threaded and now unable to be replaced), a new rear gear cable, new front gear cable housing, and a complete drive-train cleaning including the removal of the cogset and chain. One of the smaller cogs is loose but frozen onto the cog. When Keith can't remove it for cleaning and tightening, he wants to replace the whole cogset and chain, but they were new when I left home and I want to see if they will make it all the way. My only problem from the loose

Terry Fox Memorial

cog may be slight difficulty with shifting the two smallest gears. I decide to take my chances. The chain is still in good shape.

A woman approaches me in the shop while I wait. She has recognized me from the newspaper photo and asks if I will write a letter to authorities regarding the state of road conditions around Thunder Bay. She says there is a local campaign requesting immediate improvement as the area's accident rate, both auto and bicycle, including fatalities, is very high and climbing. I do not offer to write a letter while I'm pedalling across Canada, but tell her I will make their problems known wherever and whenever possible. Also, she should see some of the roads further west! They are as bad or even worse. I think Jack Layton is aware of Thunder Bay's road situation; I'm not sure about the other candidates. Certainly the state of these roads is a Canadian disgrace. I only hope I will not fall victim to them, like so many others. I'm challenged to be more prudent, to pedal with more care.

Mike delivers us back to our motel in Nipigon. We again pass the Terry Fox Scenic Lookout, an inspiration to all who pause there like we did the day before. The plinth topped with Terry's bronze stride complete with amputated leg and prosthesis is a moving reminder of what each of us can do to make a difference. Mike has made the difference for me today. Across the bay, the Sleeping

Giant Peninsula reposes in mist, jutting into Lake Superior whose endless expanse of water beckons. Next stop – riding its lonely, wild shore.

Thunder Bay presents our only security problem thus far. We are warned by local women at two libraries not to leave our locked, loaded bikes unattended outside the buildings while we take our usual hour or more for emails and updates. The final solution is a motel in a mall where a third library is located. Since emails are essential at this point in time, and camping is several kilometres from any facilities including the bike shop, we have no choice but to head for a secure place for our bikes while we tend to business. The dictates of technology! I'm wondering about carrying a Blackberry on my next trip – would it be convenient or time-consuming and possibly distracting? Would it be worthy of a toss into the bush when the batteries go dead? I'm still a Luddite when it comes to exploring archetypal Canada unencumbered with high tech stuff! Perhaps I'll change my mind by the time I reach St. John's.

But I would like to have clean drinking water as I head there. Ontario's contaminated water scares have caused several old, untreated wells in campgrounds to be declared non-potable. It's chlorine or nothing, and only a few have chlorinated their supplies. Besides the roads, this further Canadian embarrassment is a shock. Thank goodness it only happens to us in Ontario's north country, but I am very surprised it is happening at all. Hopefully, contaminated wells and other water supplies will be made safe in the near future – like the roads.

"Are you ladies from Canmore?" There's that crazy call again. We are pedalling in rare sunshine over much improved roads along Superior North, sated after a well-deserved ice cream stop. I don't believe my ears. There is some wind but the lake is lapping at our side, fairly calm. A car has passed and then pulled off into a dip on our right. Rising above boulders on the lake shore are three women, cameras cocked.

"Helen told us you were coming," they laugh as they click their shutters. Helen lives in Canmore, and one of the women is her sister. She has met Granny M during a previous visit to Canmore. I know Helen but have never met her sister, whose husband tracked us on the road yesterday on his way to Thunder Bay. They've been waiting. It's like they've struck gold! They also knew we were close because of the newspaper story. The infamous grannies ride again!

After a chat we pedal on, hoping to camp at Terrace Bay where all three women live. We arrive at the campground to find exposed tent sites and a long hike to the restroom facilities. There is no semblance of protection from tonight's temperatures, which are predicted to hover around freezing. We make much better road time when we don't get delayed by wet, cold camping. So we are on our way to a motel – again – when Peggy, one of the threesome we encountered on the road, drives up in her car. She wants to talk to us, she says. We have not met Peggy until today. She doesn't have much to offer, she says, but there are several beds in her house where she has lived by herself since the recent death of her husband. Would we like to join her for dinner and to spend the night? This is not a difficult question to answer.

Peggy's graciousness will not be forgotten. We dry our wet tents (from last night's cold camp) in her yard, use her laundry facilities, and sleep in wonderful beds. We eat her delicious chicken dinner and share a large bottle of wine with the other two women who drop by for another chat. We are now half way in both time and distance. Peggy's warm hospitality fortifies us. The maps show only 4,000 kilometres to go!

Lilacs are just blooming in Terrace Bay. It's summer solstice and everyone is wondering what has happened to their summer.

We've heard about the "hills to Marathon" for days. And they are hills! It takes five-and-a-half hours to cover eighty kilometres; there are three big ones – Two Jack Lake, Little Pic River, another lake – then continuous small ones. Rain comes whenever it thinks we might be fooled into thinking it has stopped. The good road surface holds, like Grand Père said it would. We pedal 132 kilometres to Gloria's Motel, the only truck stop and restaurant for the last 100 kilometres, and located about twenty kilometres before White Lake Provincial Park. There are no supplies or groceries en route. I carry an emergency dinner in my packs, but the thought of freezing wet camping is not luring us the extra twenty kilometres to the park.

Wimbledon tennis is on TV; even that is not inspiring. It's raining in England too. Trucks come and go all night. In the restaurant, crews of various sorts stay and eat, or eat and go. By morning the world is shrouded in white fog, and the trees are dripping with moisture. Gloria's place is across the road from White Lake – it's obvious where the name comes from. We investigate taking the bus, which isn't possible as Greyhound requires boxed bikes and where are we going to get bike boxes in the middle of nowhere? Maybe we could rent a car? This isn't feasible from Gloria's but may be possible from Wawa, 100 kilometres down the road and our destination for today's ride. Well, today's ride isn't going to happen, and I'm wondering about tomorrow and the next day. The Weather Channel is not predicting a break in this new storm system for several more days.

Duncan appears in the restaurant while we are searching for solutions with the motel manager. He offers to drive us to Wawa in his pickup if we pay for his gas. It's a deal. An hour-and-a-half later he delivers us to the car-rental gas station in Wawa, situated a few hundred metres from the town's famous Canada goose statue. Its massive wings span the width of more than an average house, but we can barely distinguish them in the fog. Wawa means Land of the Big Goose in Ojibway. The town is the gateway to Lake Superior Provincial Park, a much-anticipated jewel of my ride. After the park, the town of Montreal River and its notorious hill awaits us. One cyclist we met boasted that he can ride the hill in fifteen minutes. We didn't mention our four hour summits in B.C.

On the way to Wawa, Duncan pulls over at the townsite of White Lake for us to photograph Winnie the Pooh from our truck window. No one ventures closer to this other famous Superior North landmark. There's snow on the windshield and it's blowing, which at least dissipates the fog. Winnie looks a little sad from his perch in a wet tree trunk surrounded by drooping flowers. No honey pot here. There are many stories about the real Winnie. The one related by the women at Terrace Bay says Winnie never got further than Winnipeg, where he was taken on the train from White Lake by a local soldier on his way to war in Europe, and then let go. Winnipeg or its environs became the bear cub's new home while the soldier carried on. Who that bear called Winnie was in the London Zoo is anybody's guess. Most locals don't believe it was Winnie from White Lake. Regardless of the London bear's origin, whatever happened in London helped the soldier, and A. A. Milne's stories have cheered children for generations. Winnie the Pooh will live forever in literature, regardless of where he came from and went to.

The idea of renting a car to get us out of this socked-in wet weather system takes hold when we see that we can get our bikes into a Chevy Impala with the seats folded down and our front wheels removed. I must be more tired than I thought, because I'm not even sorry to not be pedalling this long-anticipated stretch. As long as I can see something of the park, I am happy. For an added bonus, the fog lifts as we head south on the scenic drive to Sault Ste. Marie.

Pink granite cliffs meet Lake Superior through fissured canyons carpeted with white bunchberry. A scenic hike takes us down one of the canyons to the water's edge. Off to the side there's a steep bluff with a rock shelf surfacing in the waves below. There's a sign indicating that the smooth surface of the bluff is covered with ancient pictograph symbols and figures carved into the rock. There are ropes anchored into the base of the shelf, and by venturing out onto the rocks, holding on to the ropes, one could see the colourful figures. Not today. The water's too rough and the slippery rocks too dangerous. Maybe next time. Still, it was a nice hike from the parking lot – a huge change from pedalling, even in bike shoes. And the rain and fog have taken leave of us for a few hours. Montreal Hill comes and goes. We pass several bike tourers heading west, as if they have been liberated from the weather.

Sault Ste. Marie – the Soo – is a quiet city. Drivers are not in a hurry, and people are friendly. We find an inexpensive hotel near the waterfront with a park, library, art gallery, shopping mall with movie theatre, recommended restaurant, and a bike shop located two blocks away. There's lots of museums and historical buildings to see, plus a good place to wander along the locks and do nothing. Before returning the rental car, we find an outdoor store on the edge of town and replace several necessary pieces of gear that have broken or gotten lost. This feels good. I don't regret cheating in the rental car for 250 kilometres (plus the 100 kilometres from

**City Hall,
Sault Ste Marie**

Gloria's to Wawa in Duncan's truck), and when I realize I've been pushing myself almost beyond my limits, both physically and psychologically, I know I need a whole day off. Not a shopping day, or driving, or emails, or bike shop. Just a real day off. When I tell Granny M I need this time to myself, she is speechless with anger – almost. She lets loose with a few salvos of choice attacks on my communication skills, and I don't bother to listen to the rest. Why she reacts like she does is probably indicative of her fragile state as well as mine. Down time is necessary for both of us. But she has a difficult time being convinced, and her anger punches a hole in our relationship.

I go to the movies – *The Stepford Wives* – pure nonsense, a laughable tonic. I get my hair cut. I chat with a couple in a restaurant who are from my childhood hometown in Illinois. We know the same people, although I haven't seen them in decades, and the woman knows the old farm property where I spent many summers riding country roads on my bike. An unbelievable coincidence.

When we deliver our bikes from the car to the bike shop for our general maintenance routine, there's another cyclist waiting for the bike shop to open. (I am also putting my unused extra tire on my front, keeping the worn one for a spare.) Patrick, another touring cyclist like myself, has left something behind the day before and has pedalled into town from his camp about thirty kilometres north of town to retrieve it. We immediately strike a conversation about our rides – and cycling partners. He is having a difficult time pedalling with his best friend who is less experienced than himself. "There are so many decisions to make with another person. They are petty things, like which road you take, what you eat, where you sleep, what equipment you use....yet they become so important. Almost life threatening," he laughs. Yeah, I know. We shake our heads, chuckling. "At least ride-threatening", I add. He continues to explain his predicament, "Last year I rode from Toronto to St. John's by myself. This year I'm hoping for Toronto to Vancouver. But I'm beginning to have my doubts....but he's my best friend," he repeats. His voice trails off, like he's disappointed as well as perplexed. I tell him I know where he's coming from. Granny M is unloading her bike from the car, ignoring us.

At this moment, I think Patrick and I could ride together forever and just do it. No friction, no tempers raging, no following each other, each of us doing our own thing and probably ending up the same place each night, even riding side-by-side most of the day. This kind of independence is what accompanied long-distance rides require, and I'm definitely into the concept of solo touring if that's not possible with a partner. However, in the beginning I didn't think tackling the wilds of northern Canada by myself was safe, and I was happy to have any bike alongside mine. But now that I've covered that territory, I know it's possible to go alone, and may even be the preferred way to do it.

I tell Patrick I think he's going in the wrong direction, against the wind. Mind you, this year the wind's come from every direction, so don't even think about that, I add. He is hoping it will be in his favour of course, as am I. Several months after both of our rides are completed Patrick emails:

> "Congratulations on making it to Newfoundland....I sure can relate to small and big disagreements, different plans, pace, personality. You realize who someone really is, or isn't, not to mention yourself. Wow, did Sage and I ever have some tough moments and communication slips on our way. After leaving the bike shop that morning in "The Soo" I headed back up the

road 30 kilometres to where Sage and I had made it the previous night. And as I approached our campsite, it occurred to me where what I had lost and returned to Sault-Ste-Marie to find that morning could be found. The night before my bike had dumped over setting up camp, and sure enough there in the tall grass lay those now insignificant objects. Not so insignificant however was my trip that morning, waking up in a panic, sprinting back 30 kilometres, not finding those objects but meeting you guys, and sharing some stories and good advice, then returning to Sage with a 60 kilometre pre ride and another 100 to go. I like happenings like these, choices, and life and paths, and where they lead you. I arrived in Vancouver alone, with two great friends, life friends, parted with for the moment, my first flat and the final leg of the trip, Vancouver Island, which proved to be the most beautiful, serene, contemplative part of my trip....I'm very much interested in hearing more about your book, as I too am pursuing something inspired by this journey, this ongoing journey...."

Empathetic words from Patrick. Maybe I'll have to call my book "The Journey That Doesn't End."

Granny M's anger subsides when I point out – again – that none of our itinerary is written in stone, and that I would not interfere if her need for a day off took precedence over what I thought should be happening. Compromise is the lesson of the day. She passes on the movie but together we visit the oldest house west of Toronto in the early 1800s and the bush plane museum – both tastes of early Canada history. At the art gallery there's a show of Roberta Bondar's striking photographs of Canadian National Park landscapes. Not only is Bondar, a Soo native, Canada's first woman astronaut and a physician, she also is a prize-winning photographer. I would like to take even one photo as good as hers of the parks I've been through in the past two months.

We accidentally miss the main highway out of town and enjoy a peaceful Sunday morning ride past large estates that face the St. Mary's River before hitting the TransCanada with its continuous stream of transport trucks and slim to no shoulders. Reconstruction of the disreputable old road is ongoing and tiring to ride through, yet welcome. At least future cyclists will reap the benefits. The small town of Massey's Tourist Information Centre is a lucky stop as they point us in the direction of groceries and then camping at nearby Chutes Provincial Park before heading onto a back road to Espanola where we cut south to Manitoulin Island and leave the TransCanada Highway, at least for a while. Tim Horton's at Espanola has never looked so good – it's been a long time since we've been lured for coffee and treats by that white and red Canadian icon. Even Granny M is cheered. We are pedalling without argument or flared tempers since our rest day.

What the tourist staff at Massey doesn't tell us is to beware of raccoons at Chutes Provincial Park. I'm so tuned into bears and other big dangers, I don't think about the banana in the front pannier that I leave on my bike, which is locked together with Granny M's bike around a small tree trunk near our tents. No doubt it's the banana that lures a very large round-eyed striped furry bundle to attack my pack along with my bike that it pulls as far down to the ground as possible. It's a hissing noise, almost a squeak, that wakes me. When I flash my light into its face, it slowly withdraws to the trees from where it watches me remove my pack. It growls when I slide my bike upright against the tree where it belongs. When I retreat to my tent, pack in tow, I'm not positive the raccoon will not pursue me. Eventually, the night is peaceful once again. Stars and half a moon are very bright; flashing eyes do not reappear around the bikes. In the morning I find my pack has some tiny tears from claws in the top flap, but nothing significant. However, my bike has once again been pulled as far down within the chain lock as it will go, and my handlebars are twisted to one side. Was it wanting to chew on my padded handlebars for revenge? Whatever the case, it was very quiet about it.

Manitoulin Island is a white limestone anomaly at the tip of the Canadian Shield. A series of islands connect to the mainland by causeways, plus one very old wooden swing-bridge across a narrow channel that lets shipping through from the North Channel of Lake Huron. We are making our way around another Great Lake, past Georgian Bay, across our final bout of Canadian Shield, on to Québec. It's Canada Day weekend, which means busy campgrounds and heavy traffic on the roads. There are some stretches in major disrepair again. These road conditions could become a theme song for most of Canada.

The ferry crossing between the island and Tobermory on the Bruce Peninsula takes one hour, forty-five minutes – a good rest from traffic, but not from people. We pedal the whole peninsula in one day, using side roads as much as possible, for a total of 140 kilometres to Owen Sound. We are not far from Ottawa and a real rest in a real home at Carleton Place. I'm anxious to see Pat and Henry, old friends from the opposite side of Canada where we both used to live.

Camping at Harrison Park in Owen Sound on Canada Day is something one has to experience to believe. Cheek-by-jowl campers obscure every inch of the park that meanders along creeks feeding into the Sydenham River. Bikes, scooters, roller blades, kids, dogs, etc., etc., roam the crowded lanes. Barbecues and campfires go full blast; ATV's and motor bikes take up residence wherever they unload; fireworks pop-pop all around. We find a spot, set up, and watch our front yard become home to a huge fifth-wheeler plus an accompanying four-person tent erected a few footsteps away from our own bedrooms. In our backyard is a small shelter building quickly flanked by three family-size tents and two camper-trailers.

Our neighbors in the fifth-wheel share their campfire with us, and send us off with egg McMuffins early the next morning. They camp in the same spot every year for the holiday weekend. Last year they had two middle-aged male cross-Canada cyclists resting beside them for a few days. "Who knows what next year will bring?" they laugh as we leave. "Certainly not two grannies doing what you gals are doing! Good luck!" are their parting words. It's the beginning of July – six weeks to go!

Campsites are busy and noisy, and maybe summer is here at last. The days get hotter as the hills get hillier; Canadian Shield rock-cuts and forests usher us up and down toward Ottawa. We learn that Wasaga Beach along the south shore of Georgian Bay offers only private campgrounds (Wasaga Beach Provincial Park does not have camping) that are best bypassed if possible. The crowds are rowdy

Tourist Information Centre, Kinmount

and impolite, especially to cyclists on the road. Reservations further along are necessary. Unfortunately, we get stuck and pay \$35 for a noisy dirty camp on the holiday weekend. Lesson learned! We also find the Georgian Trail for thirty-three kilometres of blissful traffic-free riding beside the bay.

At Kinmount we stop at the Tourist Information Centre housed in a renovated old railroad station nestled in flower beds on the banks of the Burnt River. At the T. I. a local named Patty arrives to check out the art displayed by local artists, and stops to ask about our biking adventures. Within minutes, she directs us to park our bikes in the back room of the station, dig our swimsuits out of our packs, and hop in her car so she can take us for a swim at her house. We do as we're told, and in a few moments are relishing a refreshing swim, complete with a glass of wine and a shower at her lovely home graced with a stunning collection of exclusively Canadian art. Patty and her husband Max have lived and travelled around the world, and now they enjoy the art of their own country. They explain all this as they give us a quick tour. I could stay for hours, but they have also told us about the movie theatre museum that Kinmount is famous for, and offer to accompany us grannies to the movies later in the evening. Also, we need to connect with Patrick at the only B&B in this town of 350 people because thunder storms are moving in for the night. Someone else making all these decisions is a REAL treat!

The movie is *Fahrenheit 9/11* which makes me think for a change; Patrick's beds are warm and dry; Patty and Max are so unexpected and so generous it is impossible to thank them enough – they know they have made a difference. Kinmount may be a tiny dot in Shield Country, but it plants a big imprint on my bike ride with a twist!

Two days later I cross a threshold into summer magic – flowers, herbs, and vegetable plants of every variety imaginable greet me. Pat and Henry, my old friends from Victoria, B.C., whom I haven't seen in four years, appear from behind all the plants and profusion of bird feeders that lead down to the banks of the Mississippi River (the one in Ontario) at the foot of their new home that Henry has built. I am fifty kilometres via the Carlton Ottawa Trail (part of the Trans Canada Trail) from Ottawa and the Ottawa River Parkway, which has to be one of the most unique paved bike paths in the world, as it follows the Ottawa River to land beneath Parliament Hill in one of the most beautiful capitals in the world. The parkway is a national treasure, worth all that rough stuff to get here.

Things are changing rapidly. I think I have seen the end of wilderness, at least for a while; I am surrounded by more people in a few hours than the whole of the past month. The weather is improving although people are still complaining it's cool for the time of year. However, I wear shorts while sightseeing Ottawa in sunshine.

A line-up of pleasure boats is being lowered by their crews through the locks between the Rideau Canal and Ottawa River, and they catch my eye from the bridge by the Chateau Laurier. I stop to watch boaters hand-winching the old gates open, letting the water level drop along with their boats, ever so slowly, as if in slow motion.

Further along, the National Gallery's collection by the Group of Seven, along with works by Emily Carr and Paul Kane, makes me feel like I'm part of the paintings – I could wade in and sit down on Lawren Harris's rocks in Lake Superior, or curl up beneath Carr's majestic cedars and have a little rest. This is the country I've just come from – I know it well! I don't know that the Museum of Civilization's current "French Settlers in Canada" exhibit is a foretaste of what's to come in Acadia, but I find it surprising that only 85,000 immigrants from France were amongst Canada's

original settlers. This is a small population compared to those who came from Eastern Europe or from Italy or Ireland or Scotland. As I well know, despite being few in original numbers, French Canada has retained its unique distinctions along with its native language – and I am about to be immersed in it. Why didn't I take more time to review my French before I left? I can only hope I will remember quickly starting tomorrow. Grand Père will meet us in a couple more days; until then I'm on my own.

Pat arranges a newspaper interview with the *Carleton Place Canadian*. The cycling grannies are becoming more famous – or infamous? Pat's eighty-two year old mom has contacted the Ottawa Sun for another interview, but they decline. We are not famous enough yet!

My new tent poles have arrived at Pat's; it feels good to shed the extra weight of the spares. Our bikes have been tuned and cleaned, once again. Bon voyage from English Canada!

Logistics

Ontario eats up 2,100 kilometres by bike plus 375 kilometres by car. I cover the province in twenty-two days, including four full rest days plus two half days off. At times the wilderness seems endless, then civilization appears after Lake Superior. Non-potable water at campgrounds along with rough roads plague Superior North, as

does magnificent scenery showing off wildlife of every description. Watch for bear and moose as well as porcupines and turtles and raccoons. Distances around Lake Superior are very long and very hilly; many cyclists claim these hills are more difficult than the Rockies. I disagree with that degree of difficulty for the hills, but the long distances will test any rider's endurance. Being prepared for what's ahead helps; don't think it's easier than it looks. Carry bear spray if it makes you feel more secure. Extra food is a necessity. Unpredictable weather is the biggest glitch to upset the best of plans.

Monday, June 14   (day 45).

Ride: Kenora to Sioux Narrows
Follow TransCanada #17A to south on #71. Peaceful wilderness ride; be ready for moose and bear. Good road surface; mostly gradual hills.

Facilities: Camping at Laughing Waters fishing camp; minimal groceries; $20 per site. Camping also available at Sioux Narrows Provincial Park or other private fishing camps; motels in Sioux Narrows. No supplies or services until town of Sioux Narrows; take groceries from Kenora as campsites and park are before town.

Total distance: 77 km.
Average speed: 20 kph.
Maximum speed: 52 kph.

Tuesday, June 15   (day 46).

Ride: Sioux Narrows to Emo (motel).
Follow TransCanada #71 and then east on #11. Western edge of Canadian Shield country; many hills.

Facilities: Emo motel. Camping at Fort Francis about 12 km east of Emo at Pithers Point Park. Several motels in Fort Francis along with shopping, banks, library, museum, murals, bike shop.

Total distance: 115 km.
Average speed: 17 kph.
Maximum speed: 45 kph.

Wednesday, June 16   (day 47).

Ride: Emo to Fort Francis to Mine Centre.
Follow TransCanada #11. Rough washboard sections of pavement crossed with tar "weather stripping". Ride past and through Rainy Lake via causeways out of Fort Francis, then into Rainy River country which is rivers, lakes, lots of water and lots of bugs! Canoe and fishing country.

Facilities: No services until Mine Centre which is convenience store and campground with showers, but minimal camping facility. Bring groceries from Fort Francis, also bug spray! Hat with bug netting useful. (Alternative for motels or better camping is to pedal Fort Francis to Atikokan, 148 km according to map measurement.)

Total distance: 106 km from Emo to Mine Centre.
Average speed: 20 kph.
Maximum speed: 46 kph.

Thursday, June 17   (day 48).

Ride: Mine Centre to Atikokan.
Follow TransCanada #11. Rough road surface again, potholes.

Facilities: Camping at Brunell Municipal Campground in Atikokan or at Dawson Trail in Quetico Provincial Park, a few kilometres off highway. Groceries, bank, post office, restaurants, laundry, and murals in Atikokan. Non-potable water at municipal campsite and in town in 2004.

Total distance: 97 km.
Average speed: 19 kph.
Maximum speed: 44 kph.

Friday, June 18 (day 49).

Ride: Atikokan to Shabaqua Corners outfitter's camp.
Follow TransCanada #11. Road surface improving. Terrain is gentle hills through trees.

Facilities: Only services en route is Kashabowie convenience store. Shabaqua Corners at busy junction with alternate Trans-Canada #17 from Dryden. Phone ahead to Oskanaga Resort and Outfitters for rooms and meals. Twin bed room with shared showers and toilets (plus bunk house beds for men) are $20 per bed; $8 for dinner, $5 for breakfast (2004 prices).

Total distance: 141 km.
Average speed: 22 kph.
Maximum speed: 56 kph.

Saturday, June 19 (day 50).

Ride: Shabaqua Corners to Thunder Bay.
Follow TransCanada #11/17 to Kakabeka Falls and downtown Thunder Bay. Kakabeka Falls a must-see.

Facilities: Camping at Kakabeka Falls and in Thunder Bay, also many motels and hotels in city. Four libraries for free Internet, but not secure for locked bikes left unattended; one branch located in shopping mall near northeast junction of Routes 102 and 11/17 which is also location of Ramada Inn Landmark Motel where one can lock bikes in room (motel is also noisy centre for partying locals). Bike shop located across town from Ramada Inn; get local directions.

Total distance: 80 km.

Sunday, June 20   (day 51).

Ride: Thunder Bay to Dorion.
Follow TransCanada #11/17. Major truck route on severely damaged road surface named the Terry Fox Courage Highway. The rough conditions indicate little to no road maintenance since Terry ran it twenty-five years ago. The Terry Fox Scenic Lookout with its nine foot bronze of Terry running on his amputated leg inspires one to keep going regardless. Amethyst shops en route; mine is eight kilometres off the road. Ouimet River and Eagle Canyon Suspension Bridge is also eight kilometres off road, the last two on rough gravel; the canyon plus bridge and camping cost $25. Long hills along north shore of Lake Superior.

Facilities: Camping at Wolf River Camp (non-potable water in restrooms but available at office building in 2004), a few kilometres east of Dorion; follow signs on highway. Only services en route, including motel, at Dorion.

Total distance: 94 km.
Average speed: 20 kph.
Maximum speed: 51 kph.

Monday, June 21   (day 52).

Ride: Thunder Bay to Nipigon.
Follow TransCanada #11/17. Road conditions improving. (I am delayed in Nipigon for returning to Thunder Bay for bike repairs.) Nipigon, the "Heart of Canadian Shield" country, is a good day's ride from Thunder Bay.

Facilities: Motels available plus camping at Stillwater Tent and Trailer Park, a few kilometres before town. Groceries, restaurants, bank in town.

Total distance: Dorion to Nipigon, 30 km.
Thunder Bay to Nipigon, approximately 115 km.

Tuesday, June 22   (day 53).

Ride: Nipigon to Terrace Bay.

Follow TransCanada #17. Road conditions good on resurfaced pavement that hugs Lake Superior shoreline. Long hills in "Superior North" country.

Facilities: Services at picturesque Rossport including accommodation and restaurants. Camping at Rainbow Falls Provincial Park between Rossport and Schreiber and at Terrace Bay (private). Motels in Terrace Bay, also groceries and bakery.

Total distance: 108 km.
Maximum speed: 47 kph.

Wednesday, June 23   (day 54).

Ride: Terrace Bay to Gloria's Motel at White Lake.
Follow TransCanada #17 for 52 km east of Marathon to White Lake. Truck traffic on good road surface until Marathon, then surface deteriorated. Huge gold mines en route; also boreal forest and famous "hills to Marathon": Two Jack Lake and Little Pic River are the longest, many other shorter ones accompany!

Facilities: Camping at Neys Provincial Park, about 30 km west of Marathon. Motels and restaurants at Marathon. Restaurant and rooms at Gloria's Motel.

Total distance: 132 km.
Maximum speed: 52 kph.

Thursday, June 24   (day 55).

Hitchhike to Wawa and on to Sault Ste. Marie.
Followed TransCanada #17 in rental car. Deteriorated road surface after Marathon, but improved after Wawa. Canadian landmarks Winnie the Pooh, A. A. Milne's fabled bear, at White River, and Canada geese statue at Wawa.

Facilities: White River services include library, groceries, restaurants, motels, campgrounds (private and provincial park); only services between Gloria's Motel and Wawa. (White River half way from Thunder Bay to Sault Ste. Marie.)

Distance: Gloria's Motel to White River: 60 km.
White River to Wawa: 90 km.

Facilities: Motels, restaurants, groceries, library at Wawa. Camping at Lake Superior Rabbit Blanket Provincial Park, approximately 30 km southeast of Wawa. Bring groceries from Wawa. Montreal hill at Montreal River long and steep. Camping at Lake Superior Agawa Bay Provincial Park near Montreal River. Camping at Pancake Bay Provincial Park (about 50 km southeast of Montreal River).

Distance: Wawa to Sault Ste. Marie: 225 km via TransCanada #17 on reasonably good road surface with long hills and very few services through Lake Superior Provincial Park.

Total distance by car Wawa to Sault Ste Marie: approximately 375 km.

Friday, June 25 and Saturday, June 26 (days 56, 57).

Rest days in Sault Ste. Marie.

Facilities: T. I., many museums, tourist attractions, lock tours, restaurants, motels, shopping, Duke of Windsor Bike Shop. The Soo is an excellent place for "rest and relaxation," and to get off and away from the bike for a few days while preparing for the second half of Canada!

Sunday, June 27 (day 58).

Ride: Sault Ste. Marie to Iron Bridge.
Follow TransCanada #17. Exit downtown Sault Ste. Marie via Bay St. East (one-way going east) to Queen St. East and follow along waterfront of Saint Mary's River to Dacey Road; turn left (north) to connect with TransCanada #17 – a quiet ride missing downtown highway traffic. Highway is the major east-west truck route and no shoulders for long stretches but road surface adequate.

Facilities: Camping at Vivian's Campground, Iron Bridge, also restaurants. Restaurants and groceries along the way at Bruce Mines.

Total distance: 113 km.
Average speed: 22 kph.
Maximum speed: 48 kph.

Monday, June 28 (day 59).

Ride: Iron Bridge to Massey.
Follow TransCanada #17. Truck traffic and intermittent shoulders with rough road. Massey T. I. helpful; get directions for next day's ride on back road (Lee Valley Road) from Massey to Espanola which avoids highway.

Facilities: Groceries in Massey, motels, Chutes Provincial Park for camping. Chutes Provincial Park has excellent facilities and beautiful walking trails along Aux Sables River; beware of raccoons in camp. Also many, many bugs!

Total distance: 102 km.
Average speed: 22kph.
Maximum speed: 46 kph.

Tuesday, June 29 (day 60)

Ride: Massey to Shequiandah, Manitoulin Island.
Follow Lee Valley road to Queensway Road on south edge of Espanola to Route 6 south onto Manitoulin Island after swing bridge at Little Current. First 30 km road surface from Espanola in major disrepair. Long hills coming onto Manitoulin Island, then flatter road along coastline. Whitefish Falls over white limestone escarpments of Manitoulin Island en route.

Facilities: Supplies and services in Little Current. Camping at Shequiandah at Batman's Camp which is well-kept campground with beach and boating on Georgian Bay (other campgrounds less attractive but same price of $10 per tent).

Total distance: 92 km
Average speed: 18 kph (headwinds)
Maximum speed: 63 kph (big hills!)

Wednesday, June 30 (day 61)

Ride: Shequiandah to Tobermory on Bruce Peninsula.
Follow Route 6 on Manitoulin Island to ferry at South Baymouth; ferry crossing is one hour and forty-five minutes. $5 charge for bikes; $11 senior passenger.

Facilities: South Baymouth is busy ferry port with numerous port-side restaurants. Tobermory is busy tourist town with all services. Camping at Happy Hearts Camp a few kilometres south of Tobermory and off the highway – follow signs.

Total distance: 57 km (plus ferry).
Average speed: 17 kph.
Maximum speed: 31 kph.

Thursday, July 1, Canada Day (day 62)

Ride: Tobermory to Owen Sound.
Follow Routes 6 and 9 which is left turn at Ferndale to Lion's Head (detour to Route 9 to avoid busy holiday traffic on Route 6 which has little to no shoulder and poor surface). Lighthouse (small, almost miniature compared to usual height) at Lion's Head Bay, which also is lovely beach area.

Facilities: Camping at Harrison Park Camp on Sydenham River at Owen Sound – ask locals for directions. Numerous motels and restaurants, all services, bike shop in town. Lunch stops along the way.

Total distance: 140 km.
Average speed: 20 kph.
Maximum speed: 45 kph.

Friday, July 2 (holiday weekend)   (day 63).

Ride: Owen Sound to Wasaga Beach.
Follow Route 26 to Meaford for Georgian Trail which is 33 kilometres of old converted rail bed with firmly packed gravel from Meaford to Collingwood and welcome relief from traffic and very poor road surface. Ask directions to trail in Meaford. At Collingwood stay on cycle path to major grocery stores in malls near waterfront. Follow waterfront cycle paths out of town, continue on Routes 26 to 92 to Elmvale.

Facilities: Phone ahead to reserve at Wasaga Pines Family Campground (tel 705 322 2727), Elmvale. Wasaga Beach Provincial Park has no camping, and private campgrounds in beach area are not recommended, even by park wardens.

Total distance: 89 km to Wasaga Beach (100 km to Elmvale).
Average speed: 17 kph.
Maximum speed: 41 kph.

Saturday, July 3   (day 64).

Ride: Wasaga Beach to Orillia.
Follow Route 92 east to Route 93; turn south and follow to Route 22; turn east and follow to Route 12 into Orillia and out to Mac-Rae Point Provincial Park which is few kilometres east/south of town off Route 12. Back roads avoid heavy traffic, include some long hills.

Facilities: All services and groceries in Orillia; lovely bakery in Elmvale for "second breakfast," T. I. in Orillia.

Total distance: 95 km from Wasaga Beach to MacRae Point Park.
Average speed: 18 kph.
Maximum speed: 51 kph.

Sunday, July 4   (day 65).

Ride: Orillia to Kinmount (B&B).
Follow Route 12 back towards Orillia from MacRae Point, then turn north on Route 44, east on Route 45. Canadian Shield country with rock cuts separating forests covering rolling hills, river valleys, some farm land.

Facilities: Few services. Carry lots of water. T. I. at Kinmount, laundry, restaurants. Kinmount House Bed & Breakfast (tel 705 488 2421). Highlands Cinema at Kinmount for latest movies.

Total distance: 81 km MacRae Point to Kinmount (possible to do long day for total 164 km Orillia to Bancroft but hills and heat may be deterrents).
Average speed: 19 kph.
Maximum speed: 40 kph.

Monday, July 5   (day 66).

Ride: Kinmount to Bancroft (motel).
Follow Route 503 to Tory Hill which is miniature postal station at road intersection; take Routes 118 to 28 to Bancroft. More hills! Bancroft is gateway to Algonquin Park and mineral/gem centre.

Facilities: Camping at Silent Lake Provincial Park about 20 km south of Bancroft. Motels, restaurants, shopping in Bancroft.

Total distance: 83 km.
Average speed: 18 kph.
Maximum speed: 55 kph.

Tuesday, July 6   (day 67).

Ride: Bancroft to Renfrew (motel).
Follow Routes 28 to 41 to 132. Renfrew is end of Canadian Shield hills, beginning of Ottawa Valley.

Facilities: Camping at Renfrew, also motels and restaurants. Pancake stop en route at Hardwood Lake where Ontario maple syrup a specialty as well as being a well-known cyclists' stop.

Total distance: 133 km.
Average speed: 18 kph.
Maximum speed: 51 kph.

Wednesday, July 7   (day 68).

Ride: Renfrew to Carlton Place (stay with friends).
Follow Routes 6 to 63 to 45 to Arnprior to 17 for short stretch to 29. Avoid busy TransCanada #17 out of Renfrew where traffic is heavy and there are no shoulders; after Arnprior there is a short necessary stretch of traffic (with shoulders) before connecting with Route 29 south/east to Carlton Place.

Alternative: take Route 20 east out of Renfrew to Castleford, connect with Route 1 and ride the Ottawa River to Arnprior, then Route 22 north/east to Route 5, then south to Carp, then north/east on Route 49 to Route 9 south to connect with Ottawa River

Parkway to downtown Ottawa. Ask locals for directions to connection with Parkway.

Facilities: all services at or near Carlton Place and in Ottawa, including bike shops. Closest camping is at Gatineau Park in Gatineau, Québec.

Total distance: 75 km Renfrew to Carlton Place.
Average speed: 18 kph.
Maximum speed: 32 kph.

Thursday, July 8 (day 69).

Rest day: Sightseeing Ottawa.

Friday, July 9 (day 70).

Ride: Carlton Place to Ottawa.
Follow Carlton Ottawa Trail to Ottawa River Parkway and motel. Ask locals for connections from Trail to Parkway via Moody Street.

Total distance: 50 km.

Québec

License plate motto: Je me souviens
Official flower: blue flag
Official bird: snowy owl

Route across Québec

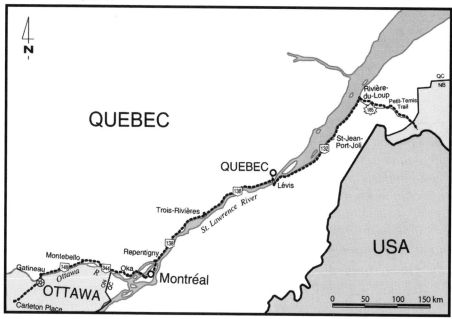

*Le Canada n'est pas le pay qui convient aux coeurs
insensibles ou aux esprits timorés."*
~ Pierre Elliott Trudeau, Address,
National Newspaper Awards Dinner, Toronto, 1972

Highlights

Bienvenue à Québec! As I pedal over the old wooden Alexandra Bridge from Ottawa to Gatineau, I can almost taste the difference between the two sides of the river. The air seems cleaner, thoughts of culinary treats to come make my mouth water, and then there's the signs – all in French. Vague memories from language courses resurface while my English stutters in protest. Directly in front of me at the end of the bridge is the Maison de Tourisme, and I am relieved when the attendant tells me in English that La Route Verte, the bike route I am looking for is clearly marked along the river. I don't need a map, and he doesn't have one anyway. Just cross the road and follow the signs, he directs.

What he doesn't tell me is that there are signs pointing to places I can't locate on my small scale map of the entire province, and the directions are confusing. While I ponder three possible routes as soon as I cross the road, a couple of cyclists resting their bikes beside a nearby picnic table are watching. I'm sure they are trying to figure out what two grannies with all our stuff on our bikes are up to.

Finally the man ventures in hesitant English, curious but cautious with his ability to communicate, "Where are you going?" I respond just as cautiously, "Montréal via La Route Verte bike paths. We are on our way to Newfoundland."

He and his partner giggle, shaking their heads in disbelief. "Where have you come from?" When we tell them where we started, they giggle again. Do they not understand my English? They exchange laughs along with some quick comments that I can't follow. "Which way to La Route Verte?" I try again. More giggles, then broad smiles.

"Suivez mois. I am Philippe, this is Giselle. We will take you." He turns his bike towards the river, Giselle follows, we grannies fall in behind. We follow paved paths that loop along parkways while narrowly avoiding trees in the middle of the paths. A pause for breath is necessary at a lookout after a steep up-hill that leaves our guides panting, while I feel like I have no breath at all. Philippe gives me

La Route Verte #1

time to re-oxygenate and explains, "About twenty kilometres to the bridge and then the highway. Okay?" Giselle smiles, shakes her head in agreement, obviously pleased with this unusual twist to her Saturday bike ride. I smile in agreement, too. We've passed several intersections with signs pointing every which way, and I am thankful for our guides who appear to know the way out of this maze. Philippe warns before the next steep up. "Get ready, change your gears," he shouts over his shoulder.

This is my first taste of Québecois hospitality. When I photograph our grinning guides at their turn-around point, there are many "merci beaucoups" and suggestions about continuing with us. "Tout le monde," Giselle sweeps the air with her hands, laughing at this joke as if the two cyclists she has just encountered are not really pedalling across Canada. I wonder if they are ever serious. Certainly they are two of the happiest people I have ever met. They turn to wave. "Bonne chance, bonne chance!" they call, still laughing. I feel a wrench – now I'm really on my own.

There is a picnic table and rest stop near the highway. Time for a snack and to regroup. I check my map, the road sign says Route 148, which is the same as the map, and then I notice – the small green and white sign with the blue bicycle – La Route Verte. This is like meeting an old friend, except I've only met this one on paper. By the time I finish Québec we will be real buddies, a few hundred kilometres of tarmac and trails cementing our friendship. It's my turn to giggle.

After pedalling a few kilometres along a wide shoulder there is a big sign, about three by five metres, reminding drivers to "share the road." "Partageons la route" spans a picture of a cyclist and a bike wheel on one side, a car wheel on the other. I have ridden more than halfway across Canada, and this is the first evidence I have seen asking motorists to share a designated roadway with cyclists, except for short stretches in towns where there usually is little traffic. (Several Canadian cities have established bike routes, but these are not the same as bicycling alerts on rural road networks.) Wouldn't it be wonderful if all provinces committed time and effort to this concept? Québec is already beginning to feel like a bit of heaven.

We follow the Ottawa River, camping in busy campsites and basking in summer weather without rain. Forays to buy groceries in local supermarkets test my French. Pedalling through bird

Share the road, Québec

sanctuaries nestled amongst riverside rushes feels like being in a different world, one suspended in nature rather than traffic. A stop at a roadside stand to gorge on delicious Montréal smoked meat piled high on delicious rye bread lets me know I'm in Québec. I photograph nondescript churches that appear almost like clockwork along the river road, and one full day out of Ottawa I phone Grand Père who will meet us with a car at Oka.

My initiation into French Canada is swift and uncompromising – I will learn to communicate, sans doute. I marvel at the realization that the French and English have managed to exist side-by-side in this big country without killing each other – yet. It's been close sometimes, I know, but in this summer of 2004 I don't feel antagonism from French locals trying to understand my foreign English, no matter what I'm attempting to say, and following the designated bike routes of La Route Verte is pure pleasure.

Oka, famous for its police confrontation a few years ago between local First Nations cigarette dealers who allegedly sold illicit supplies smuggled over the nearby U.S. border to avoid paying provincial taxes, is still a smoker's haven. I am surprised to see one cigarette shop after another lining the road into town, each one offering cheap or cheaper prices than its neighbor. Apparently the brisk business of selling cigarettes continues. Traffic is slow and congested. I'm pedalling past the line of cigarette shops followed by houses and pretty little parks with lots of flowers near the centre of town when a shiny white Cadillac, vintage 1970s, turns into a driveway on my right immediately in front of my bike. How I miss planting an imprint of my green bike on those shining white fins almost as high as my bike, I'll never know. The driver was oblivious to anything but himself and his driveway. I came very close to leaving my mark in Oka!

Grand Père is waiting by the ferry dock. He has been hanging around for about an hour he says, but he was early, and I stopped to take photographs while Granny M and I sprinted a quick eighty kilometres to get here. We are all happy to see each other. There is a train into Montréal, but only twice on Sundays for bikes, and as today has brought enticing weather, there are people and bikes everywhere. There are also bike paths throughout Montréal, but I don't have a clue how to use them. So I am grateful for Grand

Père's daughter's car and a chauffeured ride into the city, about fifty kilometres to his home.

I am also very happy to see Sue and John, along with John's brother, who will be driving sag (an accompanying vehicle that carries packs and gear) for them. They arrived at Grand Père's home two days ago from Brooklyn, New York. What a reunion we have! First there is Grand Père's daughter and son-in-law to meet, then his wife Monique who presents us with a wonderful grilled salmon dinner. This is a reunion of kindred spirits more than actual biking partners – Grand Père and Sue and I are the only ones who have officially ridden together on our U.S. tour last year, while Grand Père and Granny M and I have now done a good portion of western Canada together – but everyone else has been with us, each in their own way, so we are celebrating. The Cirque du Soleil is giving a free performance for the closing night of the Montréal Jazz Festival, and we all walk several kilometres to see it, only to be turned back by the crowd of 200,000 other people hoping for a glimpse as well. Home we trudge to watch the show on TV. After a few minutes of the show, I excuse myself for my sleeping pad on the laundry-room floor, and I am oblivious to the real world within seconds. So much for the Cirque du Soliel. We have decided to leave the city in the morning.

Montréal subways accept bikes after 10 a.m., and by then we are all ready to go, which is a minor miracle. We are now five cyclists instead of my familiar two, and one is Québecois! Sue and John pack most of their gear into their brother's car, which also carries Granny M's and my tents to lighten our loads for the subway, but the escalators are still intimidating with the weight of our panniers threatening to pitch us into oblivion past the descending moving stairs. Grand Père comes to the rescue and, with two of us holding each bike going down, we manage to get onto the trains and out of the city in one fell swoop.

Our first day's ride of ninety-six kilometres is a bit much for Sue and John as well as Grand Père after his prolonged rest. Thankfully the ride is flat along the St. Lawrence – only one small hill all day – but it is also hot. Summer is here to stay. The next day's total of eighty kilometres of still flat river riding and no rain, although it threatens in the distance, is a brief respite for the unconditioned

Sailing along the St. Lawrence Seaway

riders who then quickly acclimatize for daily rides of 75 to 110 kilometres over the next ten days.

The bike paths through Trois Rivières are incredibly rough and narrow over bridges skirting three islands in the river entering the St. Lawrence – a nerve wracking ride! Finally, we detour to a waterfront café for very tasty very French pizza (thin crust, lots of fresh veggies, local cheeses, wood-fired oven) before pedalling to a pilgrimage church and shrine at Notre-Dame-du-Cap. Tranquil gardens offer a welcome moment of peace – a real relief after dodging busy traffic in a big city with crumbling bike ways. La Route Verte has let me down today.

We could stop to pick our own strawberries, but Sue opts to buy a basket of the big red juicy berries which she somehow manages to attach to her bike without crushing its precious contents. Once at the campsite, the prize berries disappear in a blink. Camping rules the day, but everywhere is busy. We leave our tents and bikes under tarps at a rain-soaked campground about twenty kilometres from Québec City and squeeze into the car for transfer to a city motel that Grand Père locates for us.

It is the last day of the Summer Festival and we manage to catch a few street performers before being rained out. After another rain shower and a funicular ride up to the old city, we walk the ramparts to the citadel and the Chateau Fontenac that shimmers in wet flood-light. This small city, so distinctly built a few hundred years ago on cliffs above the St. Lawrence wending its way to the Great Lakes, is so European with its old brick buildings, cobblestone streets, terraces and gardens perched on steps here, or in a nook there. However, the sidewalk cafes have French Canadian menus; wine bars list Canadian award winning wines; artists' stalls feature Canadian paintings as well as Québecois works along with French Canadian crafts and folk art. And there's always the ubiquitous array of maple syrup products.

I remember my first time in Québec (travelling by car many years ago), when I thought I was in France and for some strange reason using Canadian money. Today I know the difference: Québec is not France and Montréal is not Paris; neither is Québec City simply a footprint of Europe. This is part of Canada, a juxtaposition to the

Climbing, Québec City

Québec City from ferry

English part. Each has its own distinct culture and language and history. I feel privileged to be experiencing all of it – on my bike! (And I'm still using the same money.)

We stop for second breakfasts at riverside cafes that serve crêpes with mountains of fruit, whipped cream on the side, all wonderfully created by French Canadian artisans. We are light years away from the Del Bonitas of the prairies that had only ice cream for lunch, when we were lucky. The river is widening; thunder and lightning breaks high over our heads. Québec's "Construction Worker's Holiday" has begun, which means that all construction workers (except road workers) are on the road. Phoning ahead for campsites is essential.

At Montmagny we stop at the Centre for Migrating Birds, where six injured snow geese have been rescued from their nesting grounds in the Arctic and brought to this spot on their migration route to be studied for their body growth and heat maintenance amongst other particulars. I've always been fascinated by bird migrations, especially those of the snow geese, which nest and breed in the Arctic every summer before returning to their southern wintering grounds. They are one dedicated species. We watch the French film *Winged Migration*, an award winner that I have already seen, and I ask myself why I'm taking time to watch it again when I need to be pedalling. After an hour-and-a-half of this rather bizarre interlude, we are back in the saddle.

We dodge rain showers, keeping thunder storms at bay. The wind picks up off the river which is probably twenty kilometres wide at Kamouraska, the prettiest village we have encountered. Houses and small businesses, including the village's original general store, are painted every colour of the rainbow. During lunch Grand Père and I try to remember the 1970s Canadian literary classic *Kamouraska* by Anne Hébert, which relates a tragic love-triangle and murder that actually happened in this town in the 1880s. There is also a movie of the book; I recall a French woman married to an abusive French squire from Kamouraska, and in love with an American doctor who works in the town. There are blood-drenched sleighs and frozen escape routes, sad forced marriages, and an absence of women's rights. I vow to reread the book when I get home. Afternoon light reflects off the river, and it's difficult to imagine this tranquil scene being part of such a gruesome history.

Rivière-du-Loup is our last stop on the river, my penultimate connection to Québec. I am within a few days ride from the Atlantic Ocean, a body of water first mentioned as my ultimate destination back on the Pacific coast, but one that I haven't thought about since. I've been on the road eighty days – twenty-five more to go according to my still tentative itinerary. I probably need more of a rest than I realize; it should happen in a couple more days. At the moment I need a bike shop.

Voilà! The bike shop mechanic finds a pair of stainless steel toe clips in his old stock to replace my shredded ones. One has broken completely and been duct-taped together; the other is ready to break loose. I don't use clip-in shoes and pedals because my arthritic knees and back don't agree with the stationary position they require, but finding out-moded toe clips is not easy and I feel lucky. The mechanic has his assistant fiddle with the toe clips while he dismantles my rear cogset and replaces the previously frozen and worn small ring – the one that the mechanic in Thunder Bay couldn't free – which he tells me in French will improve my shifting. The whole maneuver takes a matter of minutes. My rear derailleur also gets a good cleaning. I am very happy to get such good service – and new toe clips as well. The soles of my bike shoes are worn smooth and too slippery to hold the pedals without clips. So now I will be safer, as well as well-fed on the sandwiches I buy before

Le Petit Temis,
Québec

leaving the city – another fortuitous move.

Le Petit Témis, our last stretch of La Route Verte and also part of the Trans Canada Trail, is a cycling paradise. Built on an abandoned rail bed, the screened gravel path covers 134 kilometres from Rivière-du-Loup in Québec to Edmundston in New Brunswick, with only a four percent railway grade, of course. We get almost half way the first day, about thirty kilometres from the New Brunswick border. There is only one small drink stand until our campsite at Cabano, so our city sandwiches thick with deli meats and cheeses are much appreciated at picnic shelters along the trail – they are our last taste of Québecois cuisine except for a delicious pizza dinner in Cabano. After Cabano, we stop for photos at a stunning three-dimensional sign welcoming us to Québec. It is approximately eight metres high, flying the Fleur-de-Lys, and encasing a huge iris, Québec's provincial flower, in a circular tube at least four metres tall. Unfortunately we are going the wrong way for the sign....

But fortunately, we are in New Brunswick – the first of the Atlantic provinces we will visit. Four more to go! I depart Québec with a flat – my first puncture flat of the trip (the others have all been fractured valve sites). I've picked up a wire tack, probably from road construction in Rivière-du-Loup, where I followed

Grand Père through a mess of torn-up road rather than detouring around it. When I check my map more closely, I find we could have followed the bike route out of the city instead of a major road with construction, so the flat is my own fault. The fact that I didn't check my map shows I'm getting careless, no doubt from fatigue. When I planned the trip, I was worried that I would get too tired at the end to enjoy my ride. I'm still worried. Hopefully, a rest day coming up will help

Au revoir Québec! A bientôt, j'espère!

Logistics

Québec is so different from the western provinces that it's almost a culture shock when the border is crossed. As an introduction to Atlantic Canada there are no holds barred. Another language, different food as well as accommodation, and a maze of bike routes are just some examples of what's on offer. La Route Verte, the official provincial cycle route marked by route number signs with a bike logo, crisscrosses the province. It is my primary routing along the Ottawa and St. Lawrence rivers and into New Brunswick. Wind off the rivers can be a menace while strawberry fields, churches with elegant gardens, colourful houses and historic cities vary the landscape in a day. Cycling Québec is never boring.

Saturday, July 10 (day 71).

Ride: Ottawa to Montebello.
Cross Alexandra Bridge to Gatineau and ride east through the river park all the way to Gatineau River bridge and Route 148. Follow signs in river park or get local directions. La Route Verte "shares the route" with 148 which can be busy. Try to get an early morning departure to avoid traffic, especially on weekends and holidays. A few kilometres off the main road in Montebello is historic Chateau Montebello, now a Fairmont Hotel.

Facilities: Groceries, restaurants, motels, camping with showers at Montebello municipal campground on river.

Total distance: 84 km.
Average speed: 18 kph.
Maximum speed: 36 kph.

Sunday, July 11   (day 72).

From Montebello there are several route choices:

1. Ride: Route 148 to Route 158 and follow 158 east through Saint-Jerome and Joliette to Route 132 cutting south to cross the St. Lawrence River at Sorel-Tracy. Follow 132 along south side of the river. This is not La Route Verte and traffic can be heavy with little to no shoulders on busy roads.

Facilities: Several campgrounds, restaurants, motels along the way.

Time and distance: three to four days ride to Québec City.

2. Ride: Route 148 and La Route Verte to Route 34, direction Hawkesbury, to Route 344 at Grenville. Follow Route 344 into Oka; ferry (10 minutes) across river to Como and minor roads to La Route Verte at Vaudreuil-Dorion. Follow La Route Verte around south-east and then north-east outskirts of Montreal to cross bridge at Charlamagne. You are now on Chemin du Roy riding the north shore of the St. Lawrence, and northeast of Montreal, direction Trois-Rivières. A good map of La Route Verte around Montreal is essential. T.I. in Como and Vaudreuil-Dorion. Website is www.routeverte.com Guide book from Vélo Québec, 1251 Rue Rachel Est, Montréal, Québec H2J 2J9. Ride from Montebello to Oka is along Ottawa River through wetland reserves and bird sanctuaries. Route 344 very peaceful after earlier traffic.

Facilities: All services in Montreal. Many restaurants and motels on the way.

Time and distance: about 80 km to Oka; ferry; around Montreal about 50 km.

3. Ride: from Oka follow bike routes and/or train for bikes into Montreal. Follow bike routes and subway (after 10:00 am) to end of line, connect to Chemin du Roy for ride out of city.

Total distance Montebello to Oka: 82 km.
Average speed: 19 kph.
Maximum speed: 32 kph.

Monday, July 12 (day 73).

Ride: Montreal to Saint-Barthélemy.
Follow Chemin du Roy from bridge at Charlemagne and Repentigny (La Route Verte detours to L'Assomption on Route 344) which becomes Route 138. At Berthierville follow La Route Verte side roads to camping at Saint-Barthélemy. Ride is quite flat.

Facilities: Du Vieux Moulin campground. Groceries at Berthierville.

Total distance: 96 km (plus subway in Montreal).
Average speed: 17 kph.
Maximum speed: 28 kph.

Tuesday, July 13 (day 74).

Ride: Saint-Barthélemy to Champlain.
Follow La Route Verte through Louiseville, Yamachiche, across busy Route 40 and side roads through Pointe-du-Lac to connecting bike route through Trois-Rivières. Onto Route 138 from Trois-Rivières. Watch for rough pavement and narrow bridge crossings in city. Ride mostly flat along river. Pilgrimage church Notre-Dame-du-Cap at Cap-de-la-Madeleine just east of city.

Facilities: Camping at Camp Royal, Champlain. $15 per tent. Groceries, laundry, shopping, library, restaurants, motels in Trois-Rivières.

Total distance: 80 km.
Average speed: 18 kph.
Maximum speed: 36 kph.

Québec

Wednesday, July 14 (day 75).

Ride: Champlain to St. Augustine-de-Desmaures.
Follow Route 138 (Chemin du Roy again). There are several campgrounds just west of Québec City. I stopped about 10 kilometres west of the city and was driven (in our temporary sag car) into the city (in the rain) to sightsee. La Route Verte continues along the river on a "Corridor" to the bridge to Lévis. After sightseeing, I rode through the city on bike routes and took the ferry (10 minutes) across to Lévis. Cap-Santé en route has "the most beautiful street in Canada award" from the Globe and Mail newspaper. Québec City is a must see, at least for a day.

Facilities: Camp Canadian-Américain at St. Augustin-de-Desmaures, $5 per tent. Groceries along the way; many strawberry farms as well as restaurants.

Total distance: 94 km.
Average speed: 16 kph.
Maximum speed: 39 kph.

Thursday, July 15 (day 76).

Rest day. Sightseeing in Québec City

Friday, July 16 (day 77).

Ride: St. Augustin-de-Desmaures to Beaumont via two possible routes:

1. Going through Québec City on city bike routes, which include a steep climb up and steep descent to the ferry. This avoids the busy connection from the bridge in Lévis. From ferry, ride bike trail Parcours des Anses to Route 132.

Or

2. Follow La Route Verte, Route du Pont (Route 116), to cross bridge.Turn sharp left after bridge and drop down to the river road bike route. Follow all the way to the ferry terminal. Continue on the Parcours des Anses, and follow it to Route 132 east along the river.

Facilities: Camping and motel at Camp Beaumont which is pretty, old village with restaurants, some supplies.

Total distance: 42 km (stopped by thunderstorms).
Average speed: 16 kph.
Maximum speed: 42 kph.

Saturday, July 17 (day 78).

Ride: Beaumont to Saint-Jean-Port-Joli.
Follow Route 132 through one pretty village after another. Saint-Vallier has artisans' patisserie/restaurant for excellent lunch. At Montmagny the Centre for Migrating Birds studies snow geese whose migration corridors are nearby along the river. Saint-Jean-Port-Joli is wood sculpture centre with many shops selling sculptures of all sizes.

Facilities: Camping at La Bonnet Rouge campsite; groceries, laundry, restaurants in town.

Total distance: 88 km.
Average speed: 19 kph.
Maximum speed: 58 kph.

Sunday, July 18 (day 79).

Ride: Saint-Jean-Port-Joli to Saint-André.
Follow Route 132. Colourful village of Kamouraska en route. Flat ride along the river with wind!

Facilities: Saint-André campsite is a kayaking camp three kilometres west of town. Groceries and restaurants in Kamouraska on the way.

Total distance: 75 km.
Average speed: 15 kph.
Maximum speed: 36 kph.

Monday, July 19 (day 80).

Ride: Saint-André to Cabano.
Follow Route 132 into T. I. in Rivière-du-Loup where pick up

Le Petit Témis (La Route Verte 8), direction Edmunston, New Brunswick. Le Petit Témis is old rail bed trail on packed gravel and wonderful ride without traffic.

Facilities: All services in Rivière-du-Loup including bike shop. Take groceries for trail ride, also extra water. Camping, restaurants, laundry in Cabano.

Total distance: 100 km.
Average speed: 16 kph.
Maximum speed: 41 kph.

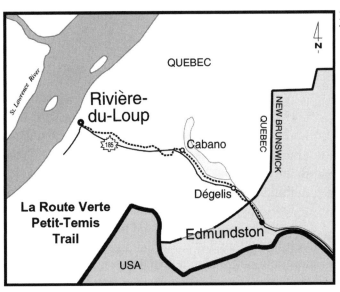

Tuesday, July 20   (day 81).

Ride: Cabano to Edmunston, New Brunswick.
Follow Le Petit Témis for more beautiful trail riding. Go through Edmunston to campground. Get local directions.

Facilities: All services in Edmunston. Iroqouis Campground on St. John River on south side of town. Take groceries from town out to campsite.

Total distance: 68 km.
Average speed: 17 kph.
Maximum speed: 42 kph.

New Brunswick

License plate motto: New Nouveau Brunswick
Official flower: purple violet
Official bird: black-capped Chickadee

Route across New Brunswick

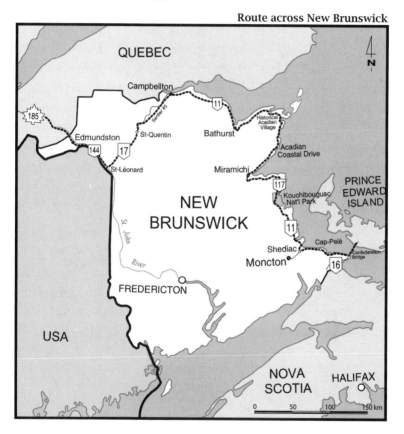

Maidens still...repeat Evangeline's story,
While from its rocky caverns the deep-voiced,
 neighboring ocean
Speaks, and in accents disconsolate answers the
wail of the forest.

~ Evangeline: A Tale of Acadie by Henry Wadsworth
Longfellow, 1847

Highlights

We find a pleasant campground on the St. John River at Edmundston, from where Sue and John will leave us to return to New York. They host a celebration barbecue – on them, they insist. They go all out. Steak and mushrooms, salmon with fresh lemon, more barbecued veggies, a gourmet salad, wine and more wine, fresh baguettes, and chocolate cake. Black flies invading the campsite are repulsed by the barbecue smoke. Everything is perfect, except for the imminent departure of my cycling friends. I am sad to see them go, yet anxious to get on with the trip. I don't have much reserve – either emotional or physical – to fortify me for the next few weeks of pedalling. My immediate goal is to reach Charlottetown, Prince Edward Island (PEI) to connect with Dennis, our group leader from last year's U.S. trip. He is guiding cycling groups on PEI, and hopefully will be able to coincide with my arrival on the island in another week.

In the morning the Brooklynites pause long enough for all of us to tour Edmundston, which is a huge pulp town,with one mill on the Canadian side of the river, and another in the U.S. across the river in Maine. The Edmundston library in a renovated church must be the most elegant library in Canada – leather lounge chairs, rich red mahogany staircases, artistic lighting featuring local artisan's work – with architecture and design unheard of anywhere else I have visited for internet access. Emailing is sometimes an intrusive task but today it's fun to write a newsy update in such remarkable surroundings. I am surprised when the librarian fetches another person to explain the computer procedures to our group in English (Grand Père, our interpreter, has remained in camp). Obviously, she is not bilingual in what is this most bilingual of provinces, according to many people I have talked to. It looks like my language challenges will continue.

By mid-afternoon the car travellers depart for the U.S.A., and I actually have some time to myself. I sit by the river to read and write, and open a bottle of wine. Relaxation is the order of the afternoon, and I obey. Tomorrow we are three riders – new group dynamics again, but familiar ones from the West, where English was the language preferred.

After we are all home safe and sound, Sue writes an email with her and John's thoughts on their Montréal/Québec trip:

"We agreed that it didn't feel like we were in Canada, although we could not come to a conclusion what it actually feels like to be in Canada. It felt foreign riding through Montréal and Québec mainly because a lot of French was spoken and the villages were very quaint. The trip would have been quite different without your guidance and Grand Père's. Safety and security was not a big issue for us. We felt like we were welcomed guests in Canada. It was a different experience from the Southern Tier [the U.S. trip Sue and I and Grand Père had done the year before] where riding in a pack was a defense mechanism. There [in the U.S.] were areas where I did not feel welcomed at all ... Glad to be able to see as much as we did in two weeks [in Québec] ... loved the rolling scenery ... Trip was physically demanding because we were not in shape and did not have enough time to acclimate to the "touring" mode ... I felt resentful for having to return to NY. Life is short and shouldn't be spent behind a desk."

I'm glad they enjoyed their bike ride in what for me is Canada's most culturally distinct province. We have talked about returning to the Maritimes and Magdalen Islands together in the fall of 2005 – another break from desk work. Our fingers are crossed that it will happen!

When we cross the border from Québec on the bike trail, there's immediate deterioration from Québec's well-maintained standard – a taste of New Brunswick's Sentiers (trails) to come. From the border to Edmundston the trail is okay, as there is no evidence of motor vehicles on the short stretch into the city, but neither is there evidence of regular maintenance for cyclists. When we try another New Brunswick designated bike route that is signed multi-use for pedestrians, horses, and cyclists, forbidding motorized vehicles of any size, we realize the value of barriers at trail heads or other access points along the routes. These obstacles have seemed a nuisance in the past, but now prove their worth. Where there are no barriers, vehicles of all sorts ignore the signs barring them from use of the trail. In fact, some joy riders on ATV's proudly "give us the finger" when they grind past, throwing dirt and gravel in our faces while churning the trail into a mess of ruts, loose gravel, big rocks, mud, dust, or whatever.

In the beginning we follow the St. John River as far as Saint-Léonard on a minor road with wide shoulders, which is a popular cycling route. Then we turn northeast to get to the coast and the Acadian Coastal Drive. I have chosen this route in favour of the interior St. John River route because I want to see the Acadian Peninsula and the Atlantic coast (actually the Gulf of St. Lawrence). To get to the coast we have to cross the northern edge of the Appalachian Mountains.

Temperatures are reaching thirty degrees Celsius and there are hills followed by more hills – a big change from flat river riding. There are also trees, trees, and more trees and no signs of civilization. There is an endless expanse of green broken by an astounding field of multi-pastel-coloured lupine wildflowers which I didn't know existed anywhere. St. Quentin is a logging town, like all of New Brunswick so far. Logging trucks give us room on the narrow road and their pine smell that lingers is a welcome change from the usual diesel fumes from big trucks. At St. Quentin we hole up at an "unapproved campsite", whatever that means as it is okay with clean restrooms and shower, then check out Sentier #5 at the tourist office. They warn that it is a multi-use trail probably not suitable for bikes, but we decide to try the first twenty kilometres anyway, and if it isn't ridable, we can get back on the road at the small town of Kedgwick. The railway grade of the trail will save us a monster hill if we can ride it. It's worth a try.

At Kedgwick we are ready for the road when the man at the health food store/café in the old rail station assures us the trail will improve, and we should definitely follow it to Campbellton, a total distance of a little over 100 kilometres he says. "It will save you that mountain on the road." Of course, there is no debate after hearing these words of encouragement.

One hundred thirty kilometres (and eight hours later) we are ensconced in a Comfort Inn to dry out and clean up. We have had everything in one day – seemingly endless rough trail with

Old train station and trail, Kedgwick

boring trees, then beautiful scenery with eighteen bridges over a meandering creek cutting through bedrock canyons. There were clouds, then sun, then rain. We went from no traffic to heavy traffic during the final few kilometres on the main road into Campbellton through construction mud in a thunderstorm. The only thing missing was crossing that mountain on the road which would have saved us the rough trail, but not much else. I want to phone the guy at the health food store and tell him to get out and ride the trail because it's so much fun – never mind the ruts and rocks and loose stuff where he'll skid and fall and probably get a puncture or two. And just ignore the ATV's spewing dusty mud in your face. I'm amazed none of us has had a flat. It's not for lack of opportunity, that's for sure.

I retreat to a motel room by myself where I service my bike and decompress in private. Next door is a Chinese restaurant that serves one of my best dinners of the trip – fresh lobster and prawns with vegetables and rice, everything prepared perfectly. The world is swirling, and it's not from the wine with dinner. So many images, and never-ending changes in the route and weather; the grande finale over mud-slicked roads; excellent Atlantic seafood I've been anticipating for a long time – I can't totally comprehend all that has happened this day. A long night's sleep with no wet tent to pack in the morning will fortify me for tomorrow. Sue and John, along with John's brother, are touring the Gaspé Peninsula by car for a day or two. They don't know what they've missed!

After the trail, our coastal road is a treat – a few moderate hills, little wind, and only intermittent spurts of traffic. We follow the Acadian Coastal Drive around the Acadian Peninsula south towards Miramichi and eventually the Confederation Bridge to PEI. Campgrounds are crowded. It's definitely summer holiday time, and we are in blue collar pulp and sawmill country. I hear bilingual speech all around me, and usually there is someone around to speak English when I need to communicate. I notice the French is different from Québecois, almost family dialects in some areas, then Acadian French when we reach the Village Historique Acadien that "strives to portray the ... great achievement of the Acadians after their deportation in 1755 ... The village strives to portray the lives of the Acadians between 1770 [when they were allowed to return to their

Village Historique Acadien, New Brunswick

Covered bridge,
Village Historique
Acadien

$20.00 FINE FOR DRIVING ON THE BRIDGE FASTER THAN A WALK

land] and 1939." The village is a remarkable reconstruction that is "staffed by interpreters in period costumes who bring ancestral customs and traditional values back to life in original buildings." My quotes are from a brochure from the village where Granny M and I spend a couple of hours; Grand Père lingers longer. The village is the first time I'm greeted with reluctance to speak English – the blacksmith doesn't want to demonstrate his skills in anything but French, and literally turns his back to me when I tell him I am English.

In the gift shop is an extensive display of books about Evangeline, Longfellow's heroine. His historic poem relates the cruel expulsion by the British of the French Acadians who had established a peaceful and prosperous political and cultural identity in their new land since the early 1600s. Not only were the Acadians French and Catholic, but by 1755 they had valuable farmland plus an enviable friendly relationship with the Mi'kmaq and other First Nations occupying the area when they, the French Europeans, first arrived. The expulsion by the British is sometimes called Canada's own ethnic cleansing, which probably isn't far from the truth and maybe explains the blacksmith's response to my being English. Some misdeeds are never forgiven, even after 250 years.

This summer is the 400th year anniversary of the arrival of Champlain and the original group of eighty French colonists who came to Acadie, their new land, and we are just a couple of days away from major celebrations at the Village Historique Acadien, as well as every village and town on the coast. The diaspora of the expelled Acadians is widespread – license plates from Louisiana and all of the eastern seaboard are parked in campgrounds and whipping by on the coast highway, which becomes the busiest traffic of our whole trip. From Cajuns to Maritimers, there's a sense of festivity; red, white and blue stripes with a yellow star of the Acadian flag fly everywhere. For many travellers, this return to their roots is an exciting, historic occasion. For Grand Père it is a magnet to stay put. He pedals with us for a day after the Village Acadien, then doesn't show for an early start from a B&B in an ex-convent where we all spend the night. I'm still trying to meet Dennis on PEI and don't wait. I had a feeling Grand Père would not finish with us. I am not surprised at this latest twist in my journey.

After I am back home, he emails:

"...After your departure I could freely change my trip perspective related to a growing desire to get in touch with the people and the country we were travelling though and more precisely to get involved with the 400th Acadian celebrations. I reminded [sic] at this specific moment that my current trip was the unconscious fulfillment of my first bike ride three years ago when I visited Louisiana and rode along the Mississippi River ... I got the feeling that trip was completed and I did not have any motivation to go further ... you get all my admiration for having realized your target. I was not so eager to do exactly the same and I just felt great to have shared your dream."

Back on the road I photograph a local Catholic church of decidedly different architecture from those in Québec. But then I've found every province to be different as far as churches are concerned. And now New Brunswick is different from Québec, not only in language, churches, and food but also in terms of attitude from people who are more friendly if speaking French, less accommodating when speaking English. The vagaries of Canada!

Lance Armstrong wins his sixth Tour de France, another historic

Bridge at Mimamichi, New Brunswick

moment. When I pedalled through his home town covering some of his training route in Texas last year just before his fifth win, I could feel his presence in the wind. He rides with me again this year. Go, Lance, go! Go, Grandma, go!

The bridge at Miramichi arises like a sleeping giant that I have to climb up and over before descending the other side. There's no time to think about it. I see there is no place for me but the road so I keep pedaling. The giant sways gently while logging trucks rumble to a stop and wait. My bike inches forward, stroke by stroke, over the giant's nose. Logs brush past and I come down fast, around the curve, all the way to the bottom. I wander off onto a side road and stop beneath a bower of trees that almost touch the ground. For a minute I wonder how I got here. Oh yes, I'm on my bike. Where to now? I ask a lady at her antique shop just off the road. Straight ahead to the water and you will find lunch, she tells me. Granny M is here now, too. We head for food – and a sense of equilibrium. No more bridges like that, please.

We inadvertently join a local seniors group for lunch. They are incredulous at our story when they ask the usual questions. Our unusual answers make their day. They reciprocate by making our day and scoop our lunch bill without telling us. When we ask the server for our bill and she tells us it's been paid, we are surprised and very grateful. We haven't been known as 'the cycling grannies' when there have been so many people pedalling with us. Looks like the title rides again.

Everywhere is packed with travellers. After our longest day of 160 kilometres, we backpedal five kilometres to the last motel room available, according to the tourist office at Cap Pelé. We don't have the energy or the time to camp in campgrounds that are full to overflowing, and rain is threatening. Pedalling with two people is easier than with three, but I'm having doubts about my energy level. I just hope I make it all the way.

The Confederation Bridge from mainland New Brunswick to Prince Edward Island opened in 1997. It is 12.9 kilometres in actual length (the van driver tells me it's almost 20 kilometres from shuttle depot to shuttle depot) and the longest bridge in the world built over ice-forming water. It is an awesome structure gently curving into the horizon while rising above the ocean as far as I can see. Cyclists and pedestrians are not allowed; there is a free shuttle van with a bike trailer to take us across. We are lucky to arrive at the pick-up depot just ahead of ten teenagers from Toronto with their bikes and camping paraphernalia so we get across quickly. The sun is shining after earlier showers and the island beckons.

Three provinces to go!

Logistics

New Brunswick claims to be the most bilingual Canadian province, and signs here are in English as much as French in most places. My route crosses the Appalachian Mountains to the coast and follows the Acadian Coastal Drive all the way to the Confederation Bridge and across to Prince Edward Island. I am in New Brunswick for the Acadian 400th Anniversary celebrations and traffic is heavy and campgrounds are busy. I ride some of the New Brunswick trail system, but it is not suitable for touring bikes as motorized vehicles have chewed up the unpaved surfaces, leaving ruts and roots and mud and dust and rocks to challenge skinny tires and lightweight bikes. There are campgrounds everywhere in New Brunswick; I have listed only a few. Some are more accessible than others. It's wise to stop at a T. I. for availability and possibly reservations.

Wednesday, July 21   (day 82).

Rest day: sightsee in Edmunston.

Thursday, July 22   (day 83).

Ride: Edmunston to Saint-Quentin.
Follow Route 144 south from Edmunston along the St. John River to Saint-Leonard, then northeast on Route 17. Nice ride on wide shoulder (popular cycling route) on Route 144; Route 17 has little to no shoulder and is quite rough in spots. Very

little traffic. Logging trucks courteous to bikes. No services or even houses for 80 km to Saint-Quentin. Very hilly! Carry lots of water.

Facilities: Lunch at Saint-Leonard; groceries, restaurants, camping, T. I. at Saint-Quentin.

Total distance: 110 km.
Average speed: 18 kph.
Maximum speed: 55 kph.

Friday, July 23   (day 84).

Ride: Saint-Quentin to Campbellton (motel).
Follow Trans Canada Restigouche Trail #5 to Route 275 for last few kilometres to Tide Head to Route 17/11 into Campbellton. Trail is rough the whole way, but very scenic, and at railroad grade so saves high climbs over the mountains on the road. Trail is in wilderness with no services or signs of civilization. Take lots of water.

Facilities: Camping at Sugarloaf Provincial Park, exit 415 off Route 11 just before Campbellton. Motels, restaurants, laundry, groceries in Campbellton.

Total distance: 131 km.
Average speed: 17 kph.
Maximum speed: 43 kph.

Saturday, July 24   (day 85).

Ride: Campbellton to Nigadoo.
Follow Route 134, the Acadian Coastal Drive. A few hills; mostly flat coastal road.

Facilities: Many lunch stops along the way. Camping at Haché Ltée, $20 per site for two tents. Groceries, restaurants, laundry in town.

Total distance: 102 km.
Average speed: 21 kph.
Maximum speed: 48 kph.

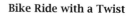

Sunday, July 25   (day 86).

Ride: Nigadoo to Tracadie-Sheila (motel).
Follow Route 134. Watch for bike route through Bathurst to avoid heavy traffic and no shoulders (follow other cyclists veering to the right onto paved sidewalk-bike trail as you come into town). Flat coast riding. Plan for at least an hour if you want to tour the Historical Acadian Village near Caraquet.

Facilities: Camping at Tracadie-Sheila, also motels, restaurants, groceries. Lunch stops along the way, including Historical Acadian Village.

Total distance: 127 km.
Average speed: 20 kph.
Maximum speed: 53 kph.

Monday, July 26   (day 87).

Ride: Tracadie-Sheila to Baie Ste. Anne (guest house).
Follow Route 11 to Miramichi, then Route 117, both routes continuing the Acadian Coastal Drive along Gulf of St. Lawrence. Very high bridge at Miramichi – only place to ride is on the pavement, so just keep going – swing left below bridge for town centre and restaurants, etc. and to connect with Route 117.

Facilities: Free email access at Neguac library. Lunch stops at Neguac, Miramichi. Campgrounds near Baie Ste. Anne off road on the beach. Guest house in Baie Ste. Anne, also restaurants, some groceries.

Total distance: 133 km.
Average speed: 19 km.
Maximum speed: 39 kph.

Tuesday, July 27   (day 88).

Ride: Baie Ste. Anne to Cap Pelé (motel).
Follow Route 117 into Kouchibouguac National Park. Can stay on Route 117, which changes its number several times as it follows the coastline. To save time, connect with Route 11

at Kouchibouguac town, direction Shediac (still going south). Route 11 is heavy traffic with narrow shoulder and very little shelter. Most services are off road. Have plenty of water with you. Onto Acadian Coastal Drive, Route 133 at Shediac to Cap Pelé.

Facilities: Food stop at Rexton, Shediac, then small towns on coast. Camping, motels, restaurants, some groceries, T. I. at Cap Pelé; also at Shediac, about 20 km before Cap Pelé.

Total distance: 160 km.
Average speed: 20 kph.
Maximum speed: 39 kph.

Wednesday, July 28 (day 89).

Ride: Cap Pelé to Hunter River, Prince Edward Island [B&B]. Follow the Acadian Coastal Route which changes its number several times and can be misleading – get local directions where questionable. Follow along the coast until Confederation Bridge looms on the horizon. No bikes or pedestrians are allowed to walk or ride across. Pick-up depot is large building on right just after junction with TransCanada #16. In high season, there is a number system for getting on the shuttle van with bike trailer that takes you across the bridge free of charge. The shuttle is for pedestrians as well as bikes, and can be busy with groups of cyclists coming onto PEI. Take a number from inside the depot and wait your turn. Packs are unloaded and stored when possible beneath the bikes on the trailer or in the van; bikes are strapped upright on the trailer. See PEI Logistics for remaining day's ride.

Facilities: Nothing much for shelter until the depot at the bridge. Carry water and snacks.
Coffee stop at Murray Corner.

Total distance: 25 km Cap Pelé to Confederation Bridge. Bridge crossing takes about 30 minutes. Wait time is guaranteed to be no more than two hours.

Prince Edward Island

License plate motto and logo: Confederation Bridge
Official flower: lady's slipper
Official bird: blue Jay

Route across Prince Edward Island

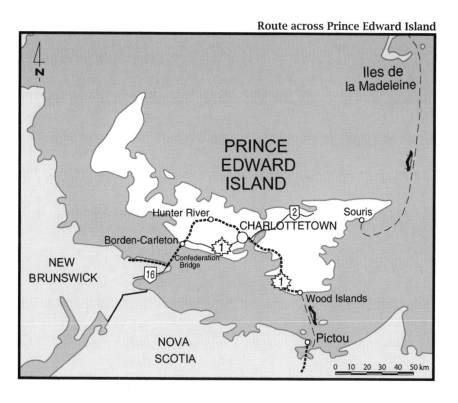

Home of the Confederation of Canada in 1867, Lucy Maude
Montgomery and *Anne of Green Gables* in early 1900s, potatoes
and red dirt forever.

Highlights

It seems strange to call this small island a province, especially when comparing it to all those days and days of wilderness in Ontario, or the western prairie provinces – or the mountains of B.C. – or the mighty rivers of Québec. However, red dirt and potato fields lend their own individuality to this wee province on an island roughly half the size of Vancouver Island on the opposite coast of Canada where we began our trek eighty-nine days ago.

For cyclists, PEI's Confederation Trail is the piéce de résistance – over 350 kilometres of "rolled stone-dust surface" cover an abandoned railway for a ride over the entire island, 270 kilometres reaching from tip to tip. The trail is dedicated to cyclists and hikers with barriers erected at every road junction or other access points to prevent motorists of any kind from entering the trail. Apparently snowmobiling is allowed in winter, so the barriers are probably opened, but for now we have to negotiate our loaded bikes on foot through the frequent obstacles. However, after the open destruction of the trails in New Brunswick, this is not an issue for us.

Thunderstorms threaten and we head for cover. A woman working in a nursing home just off the trail directs us to her mother's B&B just up the road. As soon as I leave the trail I realize the comfort of the railway grade despite several gradual hills I have managed without much strain. On the road it is only three kilometres to the B&B but two abrupt climbs push my limits. The B&B is a wee heritage home built in 1885 and crammed full of vacationers. There are ten of us for one bathroom, no doubt reflected in the price of $45 for our double room. A visiting Toronto family with three young children share our breakfast table and the inevitable questions start. I find I'm teary eyed – I can hardly believe my answers myself. This is an emotional morning, a pause in an idyllic spot that lets some reality sink in. I really have pedalled most of Canada and I really am very close to going all the way!

There are many photos taken of the cycling grannies before we leave. Cindy, our host, attempts to arrange TV coverage for us and we depart with the possibility of meeting the local station at the

Province House, Charlottetown

Tourist Information Centre in downtown Charlottetown at 2:00 p.m.. We arrive on time, but the TV people don't show. Still not famous enough! I don't doubt that if we were cycling for a national cause (Granny M is raising money for a local church project back home), we would have more clout with the media. Riding for its own sake doesn't count. Why riding for a charity makes such a big difference, I don't understand, and I know that my commitment to establishing my route is enough personal justification for my ride. What has been truly impressive is what I have seen of Canada from many different perspectives – a reward I didn't expect, and one that has nothing to do with raising money for over-subscribed charities – or exposure in the local news.

Charlottetown, PEI's capital city, is where it all began. Confederation meetings at Province House in 1867 produced Canada, ironically without PEI until the independent island finally joined in 1873. We pedal into historic downtown, find an inexpensive motel for a couple of night's rest, and visit a bike shop for tune-ups and drive-train cleaning. I also replace my worn slippery bike shoes with hopes that the burning sensations on the soles of my feet will dissipate despite the now constant heat from the road. The shop owner invites us for a ride around town at 5:30 the next morning. He's established an early morning routine along with a local newspaper reporter who is training to ride the Confederation Trail. He thinks she will be interested in doing a story on us.

It's early, but I get up knowing I can go back to bed after the ride. We follow our leader through deserted downtown, riding the boardwalks around the harbour illegally. I stop for a photo of the sun rising over Confederation Square on the waterfront. This is where various delegates landed on this obscure and little known island to negotiate the agreement that brought the English territories together under the crown of England, which also had received French Canadian territories from France after Britain's defeat of France in the Seven Years War. Once Canada's trans-continental railroad was established in 1885, all of English Canada united against French Canada while French Canada united against the English, which to this day forms a mutual exclusion, seemingly to everyone's benefit, although many will not admit it. The newspaper reporter asks a lot of questions about our trip, but not for an article. We are excluded once again, perhaps because we are "from away," as they say regarding non-PEI natives. But there are thousands of cyclists on PEI, literally, and we two grannies are just two more of them. There are probably as many good stories to tell as there are riders to tell them.

I try to find enough time in my schedule to get to the Magdalen Islands, which I told Jack Layton would happen if at all possible. I could take three days to allow for the six hour ferry ride to get there and then back again, and have one day to explore the islands – not enough time to make the expense and time of the ferries worth it. Besides, most of the islands are totally French which Granny M has difficulty with, so I decide I will return at another date with enough time to enjoy the islands, both the French and English ones. I'll send Jack a postcard whenever I get there.

My day off is a celebration of 7,000 kilometres on my cyclometre, accrued over ninety days since I left Vancouver Island. Dennis and I meet for a drink, another happy reunion. He is astounded at my statistics. He is leading "luxury tours," as he calls them, and the five-star hotel where we meet is certainly many steps above my little motel across town as well as camping across the continent in both the U.S. and Canada. His company caters to wealthy clients who want a week's holiday with no worries and lots of comfort – something they can well afford. I could probably afford it too, if I wanted to spend what it's cost me to ride across Canada for a week's ride poking around PEI. "I'm up for more adventure and challenge," I remind him. We both laugh and reminisce about our U.S. ride last year, especially the diverse personalities of our group. We mourn the fact that Grand Père and Sue have missed our reunion by mere days. "I've had similar diversities to last years' group with all my different riders this year," I tell him. It's great to talk with an experienced cycle tourer; a little like meeting Patrick in Sault Ste. Marie, oh so long ago. Too bad we don't have more time. We discuss cycling on the Magdalen Islands. "Maybe next year," he says. Yeah, me too. Sue and John are hoping it's a possibility also.

My second day off includes a couple of hours reviewing Canada's history at Founder's Hall and Province House, visits that provide helpful insights to this diverse country with so much history in each province. Granny M connects with old friends now living near Charlottetown who give her a mini-tour of the island, including Anne of Green Gables territory. Now we are tourists without wheels.

After my rendezvous with Dennis, I walk to an historic house on the waterfront for a classical music concert of flute, guitar, and piano – the only taste of my kind of music I've enjoyed on the entire trip. The concert is soothing, a reminder of my other world that I've forgotten exists. I've often wondered if a little Mozart by Walkman would be a welcome addition to my gear, but haven't been convinced to carry the weight or believe I'd have enough listening time to make it worthwhile. Maybe I'll change my mind when I rethink high tech accoutrements after I get home.

Next day is Sunday, August 1, a civic holiday everywhere but PEI (and Québec and Newfoundland). We pedal to Wood Islands ferry terminal dodging rain showers, and seventy-five minutes later are in Nova Scotia, our penultimate province. Hard to believe I'm this close to the end! I'm feeling rested for a change, unsure of the challenges ahead. I know Newfoundland has a lot of hills, but I'm trying not to think about them.

Logistics

No Prince Edward of England has ever had much to do with this island namesake. However, his title is permanently attached to the mound of red dirt affectionately known as PEI.

Initially settled by as many French and Scots as English, PEI today boasts a mixture of names and cultures, and shows off its home of the Canadian Confederation to thousands of tourists every year. Cyclists flock to the island's Confederation Trail, a rejuvenated railbed that covers 270 kilometres from one tip of the island to the other, with a total of 350 kilometres of rolled stone-dust surface trails extending from the central railbed. PEI's roads are hilly, narrow, and busy; riding the trail is a treat of gentle grades, wide tracks, and no motorized traffic.

Wednesday, July 28   (day 89); a continuation from New Brunswick.

Ride: Borden-Carleton on PEI side of Confederation Bridge to Hunter River (B&B).

Follow Confederation Trail to Hunter River exit and B&B on Route 2. Enter Confederation Trail at road junctions at Borden-Carleton. This section of trail is hilliest part of the island; hills on Route 2 are steeper and shorter.

Facilities: Restaurants, motel, camping, shopping, some groceries at Borden-Carlton. B&B and restaurants near Hunter River. Some snacks along the way.

Total distance: 52 km Borden-Carleton to Hunter River.
Average speed: 17 kph from Cap Pelé, New Brunswick to Hunter River, PEI.
Maximum speed: 42 kph for total distance.

Thursday, July 29   (day 90).

Ride: Hunter River to Charlottetown (motel).
Follow Route 2 for few kilometres onto Confederation Trail. Spur of trail into Charlottetown is rough gravel that crosses major road junction on an angle. Ask locals for directions.

Facilities: All services in Charlottetown including MacQueen's Bike Shop, free Internet at library. Closest camping is at Stratford southeast across bridge and off TransCanada #1.

Total distance: 38 km.
Average speed: 15 kph.

Confederation Trail, Prince Edward Island

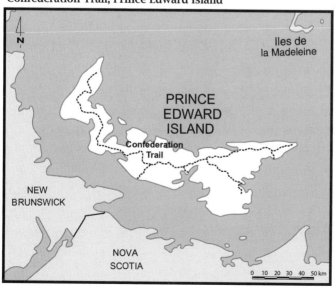

Maximum speed: 40 kph.

Friday, July 30 and Saturday, July 31   (days 91, 92).

Rest days: sightsee in Charlottetown and on island.

Sunday, August 1   (day 93).
Ride: Charlottetown to Wood Islands.
Follow TransCanada #1 with wide shoulder; ferry 75 minutes to
Pictou, Nova Scotia.

Facilities: Camping and groceries near Wood Islands, also along
the way from Charlottetown. Restaurants, motels available. Ferry
charge is $16 for bike and passenger combined.

Nova Scotia

License plate motto: Canada's Ocean Playground
Official flower: Mayflower
Official bird: osprey

Route across Nova Scotia

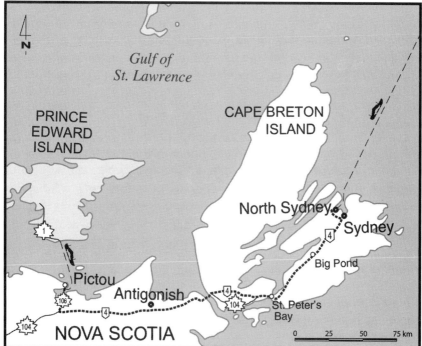

Cape Breton in my dreams...
You never let the hard times take away your soul.
~ Rita MacNeil, song Home I'll Be

Highlights

It's Sunday in Nova Scotia and all stores are closed. There's a convenience store about ten kilometres from the campground that may be open; there's also a nice restaurant a short walk up the beach. "Check it out," the campground attendant advises. We are camping at the birthplace of New Scotland, settled by Scots in 1773, just after the Acadians were allowed to return to their homes nearby.

It is a lovely restaurant with spectacular views towards PEI across Northumberland Strait. Wedding reception guests and others mill about, glide on platform swings, and watch the sun set. The beach is littered with Adirondack chairs, sand castles, wildflowers poking through the sand. Back at camp it is unbelievably warm all night. We even have dry tents in the morning.

The next day is Monday, Nova Scotia's Natal Day civic holiday, so everything is still closed. I find some emergency snacks in my packs for breakfast before pedalling into heavy traffic on the main highway which we exit as soon as possible to follow the old Route 4 through hilly farm country with little traffic, but no services. Our first stop for nourishment is ninety-two kilometres later at Antigonish – too long without food over demanding terrain in thirty degree Celsius heat! I'm reminded of pedalling in Europe, where supplies have to be purchased before shops close for two or three hours every afternoon. Nova Scotia is not open for business on Sundays or holidays so buy supplies on Saturday. I learned this lesson too late.

We pedal past New Glasgow, and stop for a rest on the steps of a rural Presbyterian church where the cemetery records the deaths of several Scottish children in 1845. One can imagine the harsh winter or sickness that spread through the settlement, possibly not much different from old Scotland across the sea. Antigonish is advertising its Highland Games. Cape Breton Island is linked to the mainland with a causeway that is easy to pedal until the island road ascends into the sky beyond the Tourist Information Centre. I push my bike up, past Scots and Irish names everywhere.

Pictou beach

Lucy camps beside us, her lilting Scots accent matching the territory. She has pedalled on her own from her Canadian relatives' home near Toronto through Halifax, and is now heading for the Cape Breton Highlands, which I am bypassing. We share cycling tales and find we have both been rescued by kind folks in Kinmount, Ontario complete with an escort to its famous movie theatre/museum. Maybe capturing cyclists is a trademark of those townspeople? Lucy emails when she gets back to Scotland:

"The Cabot Trail was magnificent and I got beautiful weather to do it in. The ups were really hard work (but I managed to pedal most of it) but well worth the effort – the views were beautiful and the downhills exhilarating – I'm sure I looked like a Cheshire cat on the way down ... hope you managed to complete your journey without mishaps."

We cyclists are a breed unto ourselves: independent, and hard working, seeking our just rewards. Nothing else is like it!

One night we are treated to authentic Nova Scotia fog for supper. It swoops into our campsite where we have camped for the view – before it disappears. The day has been another thirty degree scorcher until we descend into a bay and a temperature change that feels like we have ridden into a freezer. The campsite is cool, the fog cooler, the moon bright around midnight, the tents dry in early morning sun – a hodge-podge of weather like the people and languages and cultures we've pedalled past.

Granny M and I continue to follow the old Route 4 up Cape Breton Island towards Sydney and our goal, the ferry to Newfoundland. We avoid the main road as traffic is very heavy and Acadian flags are prominent again. Their 400th anniversary has brought thousands of visitors to Nova Scotia as well as New Brunswick, although the Scots still seem to be the most prevalent influence in this part of the province. Still, there are many German signs and names as well. Nova Scotia is a true Canadian mélange.

Just when I despair of finding a place for lunch before dinner time, Rita's Place appears on the road. When I walk through the door, Rita MacNeil's singing drifts from surround sound throughout her old home built around an old school house. Now it's a restaurant. Big Pond where she grew up is just up the road. Rita is another Canadian icon, both in voice and her contributions to the Cape Breton music of her native land. I remember her Christmas tape from many years ago, when my daughter was still young enough to sing along with her silly mom in the car on our way to Christmas shopping. Rita is joy and down-home love. Her clam chowder fills my empty stomach – she makes me happy again!

Rita's MacNeil's schoolhouse-home-restaurant

When we arrive in the outskirts of Sydney, we are confronted with bike-stopping construction. Workers tell us we can walk our way through following the almost non-existent car lane. At last we reach a sidewalk around the big ditches and Alan, a local cyclist also making his way through the construction, asks if we need directions. Granny M needs another adjustment of her derailleurs (since Charlottetown), so Alan leads us to Me Buddy's Bike Shop where Don, the owner, doesn't charge for the mechanic's adjustments, and offers us soft drinks and chips while we wait. Alan asks the usual questions and decides to call a reporter friend in another attempt to get us in the local news. The friend is busy with a deadline and can't do our story. I'm surprised at how many casual acquaintances respond to our stories by calling the media. Is this a sign of our high-tech news world? I'm not surprised at the results. I don't know how the people making the requests feel when they are given the cold shoulder. I wonder how many more times this will happen in the next couple of weeks?

We spend the night in an affordable Sydney motel recommended by the bike shop owner when we find that accommodation closer to the ferry is either too expensive or fully booked. So we have an early start for our last province as the ferry terminal is a twenty kilometre ride before our 9:00 a.m. check-in in the morning. We really have only one more province to go!

Logistics

Nova Scotia's Scottish heritage vies with its French Acadian history, 400 years of which are being celebrated in New Scotland during 2004. Traffic is the heaviest I've experienced across Canada, and I head for the less travelled roads as quickly as possible. Old Route 4 parallels new TransCanada #104 as far as Cape Breton Island, then branches off to the east side of the island to Sydney and the ferry to Newfoundland. All of the route is hilly with key-hole views of charming harbours in picturesque bays with pastoral scenes in the background. I know I am having only a brief encounter with Nova Scotia, but these micro views and historic anecdotes wherever I turn surprise me. My favourite sign on Cape Breton advertises the island's "Tapestry of Seascapes and Cultures," an apt description.

Monday, August 2 (day 94).

Ride: Pictou to Antigonish.
Follow TransCanada #106 south to #104 east to Route 4 at New Glasgow. TransCanada very busy; Route 4 very quiet but rural hilly farmland and no services. Antigonish famous for life-size wooden sculptures through-out town.

Facilities: Camping last night at Caribou-Munroes Island Provincial Park near ferry terminal on Pictou Harbour. Groceries at Wood Islands, PEI, and in Pictou. All stores closed in Nova Scotia on Sunday. Bring supplies from PEI on weekends. Restaurants, motels, inns in Pictou. Camping and laundry at Widdens Campground in centre of Antigonish. $27 for one site for two tents. Groceries, restaurants in town.

Total distance: 92 km.
Average speed: 18 kph.
Maximum speed: 55 kph.

Tuesday, August 3   (day 95).

Ride: Antigonish to St. Peter's.
Follow combination of Route 4 and TransCanada #104 (follow signs) to causeway to Cape Breton Island, then Route 4 east to St. Peter's town on St. Peter's Bay. Carry snacks and extra water.

Facilities: T. I. at causeway road junction, also snack and water. Few supplies until St. Peter's. Camping at Battery Provincial Park just beyond St. Peter's town. Take groceries from town. Restaurant in town.

Total distance: 114 km.
Average speed: 18 kph.
Maximum speed: 57 kph.

Wednesday, August 4   (day 96).

Ride: St. Peter's to Sydney (motel).
Follow Route 4. Many hills! Rita MacNeil's Tea Room on Route 4 near Big Pond a highlight.

Facilities: Motels in Sydney, North Sydney near ferry terminal, also at Little Bras d'Or west of North Sydney. Camping north and west of Sydney. All services in Sydney; Me Buddy's Bike Shop. Ferries to Newfoundland leave from North Sydney.

Total distance: 90 km.
Average speed: 17 kph.
Maximum speed: 55 kph.

Thursday, August 5   (day 97).

Ride: Sydney to North Sydney.
Follow old road – ask locals for directions. Ferry to Port-aux Basques, Newfoundland takes six hours.

Facilities: ferry is $12 for bike, $36.75 senior passenger. Reservations accepted.

Total distance: 24 km (time 1 ½ hours).

Newfoundland & Labrador

License plate logo: Province Map
Official flower: pitcher plant
Official bird: Atlantic puffin

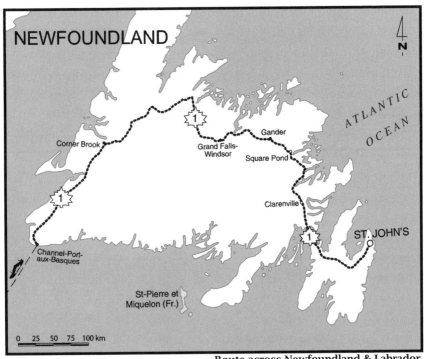

Route across Newfoundland & Labrador

Going up the highway
*   Pedalling to St. John's*
Watching for a moose
*   To end me ride.*
                    ~Janice Kenyon

Highlights

The ferry from North Sydney, Nova Scotia to Port-aux Basques, Newfoundland takes seven hours. It's a surprise to find free Internet access on the ship, and I write a brief email update – perhaps my last? Our bikes are the only two-wheeled machines on the car deck. We join a tour of the ship's bridge along with five other tourists and watch "The Rock" rise out of the sea, complete with patches of snow on the mountains. Closer to port little boxes sprout on the rocky shore; gradually they materialize into houses on bare land. I am struck by the absence of trees. It's exciting to watch Newfoundland emerge; I can't help but spill the beans about the cycling grannies' plans to cycle across this looming island of mountains and rivers and ponds and moose. Everyone, including the captain, catches our excitement, but there are no media threats at sea!

We disembark at 5:15, Newfoundland time, and pedal into a forty kilometre per hour headwind. Camping in a provincial park without showers is at least ten kilometres up the road, and we do not have groceries with us. It's not difficult to turn into a motel on the edge of town where the woman desk clerk wants to reward our cycling efforts with a free room, but is allowed to give only a "senior's discount." She is awestruck at our achievement thus far, almost as if she doesn't believe it's possible. It seems that Newfoundland hasn't seen many cross-Canada women cyclists in the past, which makes the natives just as curious about me as I am about Newfoundland. I've pedalled 7,450 kilometres to get to this outermost piece of Canada which I quickly learn is not Newfoundland, but Newfoundland and Labrador, and not a Maritime province, but rather an Atlantic one. Cariboo casserole – my first – for dinner seals my fate. I will pedal across this rock to discover what makes it so unique in the eyes of so many. My flight home from St. John's is in ten days time; road distance Port-aux Basques to St. John's is 905 kilometres.

After the cariboo casserole, I hit the sack in record time. Two motel nights in a row make for easy unpacking and redoing. I check my bike carefully and add air to both tires. I'm ready for Newfoundland!

I'm asleep about five minutes before an incredibly loud explosion rocks the room. My first thought is maybe the fan by my head has blasted into a thousand pieces. Granny M whispers loudly, "The bike!" I flip on a light to see my front wheel resting on its rim, and the tire I have just pumped up blown completely off the wheel. When I take everything apart, the tube falls out in shreds. It has a fifteen centimetre split in it, which I finally decide must be from fatigue. I get the tire back on the wheel, a new tube in place, pump it up again, get the wheel back on the bike where it belongs, and go back to sleep. I don't hear another peep out of either tire for the rest of the night, or the rest of the trip.

Port-aux Basques takes its name from Basque settlers who came here to fish several hundred years ago (c.1500). One of Newfoundland and Labrador's boasts is that it is the youngest province of Canada, but has a culture already older than that of the confederation it joined just a few decades back. Several centuries of contributions from French, English, Irish, Basque, and Viking settlers add to the province's much longer Aboriginal occupation to make up its diverse heritage. France still holds sovereign rights over the tiny islands of Miquelon and St. Pierre just minutes by ferry off The Rock's south coast. Acadian anniversary celebrations continue to follow us.

Our first day's ride totals 137 kilometres before we find a place to rest our weary bodies. Scenery is magnificent for the first part – needle-like spires of rock usher us up and into hills gradually covered with trees and more trees. I've been warned about endless trees along the inland route, but there is only one road across Newfoundland and that's the TransCanada Highway, or T.C.H. as it's called, and so far it's anything but boring. Also, the road surface and shoulder are the best we've encountered in Canada! Crashing noises in distant trees make me think of moose, but we don't see them. When we stop to buy food to take with us to the provincial park we are heading for, it is already 6:00 p.m., with thirty more kilometres to the park. The campground will probably be full, Jason at the gas station convenience store informs us. We are at the town

Long and winding roads, Newfoundland

of St. George's and its Blueberry Festival is in full swing. Jason has a suggestion. He can call Tom who has a B&B down the next side road. "Come over here. I'll show where to turn," he points to a car entering the highway at the bottom of the hill. "I'll phone and see if he has room. I think that's your best bet for tonight. Everywhere is full because of the festival."

Tom is from Connecticut in the U.S. He is building a B&B which will eventually be a hunting lodge for his American hunting compatriots. He is the last person I expect to meet in Newfoundland and Labrador. He is ex-Navy (U.S.), a Vietnam veteran, and a moose hunter. He serves us barbecued pork chops for dinner and between us we manage a couple bottles of French wine. His home is a work of art, built mostly by himself, but with some help from the locals he admits. In the morning he sends us off with a hearty breakfast, wishing us a good journey. He is not particularly impressed by our cycling efforts. He prefers ATV's. We are not particularly impressed by his hunting prowess or his war stories, but he had a safe haven for the night, and we are grateful.

Jason from the gas station phoned to check on us while we were having dinner. Now that's Newfie hospitality!

We set off in a light drizzle that doesn't let up. Visibility is poor as we climb over the spine of Newfoundland's western mountains, but I can make out tundra-like peat fields and a few wildflowers. I just wish I could see them properly. The rain comes harder and traffic is frightening, especially on slippery downhills. We pedal seventy kilometres before there's a place to stop, by which time we are soaked. My rain gear has kept part of me dry, but I'm dripping from everywhere as I peel off layers in the restaurant. I am cold enough to retrieve my fleece jacket from my pannier in the rain. Customers in the restaurant stare. It's true – we are an anomaly.

"This is it. I'm looking for a ride," I sputter to Granny M who agrees with me. Pickup trucks dominate the parking lot; passenger cars are rare in this part of the world. Our server offers to ask around for us. Finally the restaurant owner agrees to take us as far as the bus station in Corner Brook where he lives. "About twenty kilometres down the road," he says. And it is down, into the Humber River Valley, the best scenery so far, but still partly hidden in rain clouds. The bus requires boxes for bikes, of course. Where have I heard this before? Another friendly man offers to take us another twenty kilometres as far as Steady Brook, which he says is a good place for rides as it's a junction for traffic from Labrador, the south, and Port-aux Basques. Granny M and I imagine hitching a ride all the way to St. John's on a transport truck. That's what pedalling in rain can do to one's morale.

At Steady Brook the rain eases by late afternoon. We find a room at a ski chalet which is part of Marble Mountain Resort, "the ski gem of Atlantic Canada," and a big surprise to us. We can see ski runs disappearing into layers of fog hanging over the mountain, and chair lifts that ascend into white oblivion. Next morning the fog still hovers but the road is dry and we get back on our saddles. Thoughts of hitchhiking disappear with the rain. Considering the possibilities for return to this picturesque area to ski takes my mind off the hills I have to pedal. "Just get to St. John's," jangles in my head, over and over.

The man who gave us a ride to Steady Brook had his three kids in his truck, and they all eagerly told us about their four-month North American circuit in a motor home back in 2001. Dad said

**Marble Mountain
Ski Resort,**

it was a family trip to educate and discover, and obviously none of them have forgotten the experience. We could relate to each other's travels, but I was stumped for an answer when the oldest boy, now twelve years old, posed a very serious question when he asked, "What made you ride your bike across Canada?" He really wanted an answer, a concept he could identify with and not a vague excuse about doing it "because of the challenge," whatever that means. I mumbled something about discovering Canada from a bike being far different than any other form of travel, and more exciting. "Yeah, but Canada is so big," he tried to reason with me. "It sure is, I can tell you that for sure," I wanted to reassure. He was still pondering when we unloaded our bikes. "Don't think I'd ever do it," he concluded, determined to take a stand. Maybe he's got a point, but I wanted to encourage him. "Really, it's a great way to see your country!" We shook hands to say goodbye. I could tell he wasn't convinced.

I think about "why" while I pedal through hours of nothing except scrub spruce, a few ponds, occasionally a lake – at least what I call a lake, probably still considered a pond in Newfoundland. Distances disappear in trees and hills; Tim Horton's appears every 100 kilometres or so and we stock up. I've taken to the idea of getting Tim to sponsor us; I've given him so much business that I am practically walking – oops – pedalling chicken with bacon baguettes and fruit surprise muffins. Hills are long and sometimes endless, but it's amazing how they get swallowed as we grind up, then spit out on the coast down. The day after Steady Brook is my 100th day on the road, and with the end almost in sight, I'm trying to grasp the meaning of this trip. Partly it was the challenge – to see if I could do it, but mostly it was to see Canada from the inimitable perspective of my bike. There really is nothing else that I have done that compares with my adventure of the past three months. All those peripatetic clicks on my cyclometre in Europe – even above the Arctic Circle in Norway – lose significance in the heartlands of Canada.

We camp at Fort Birchey Campsite where a café features huge burgers and homemade apricot pie. We meet a cyclist from Maine who bivouacs in the bush rather than pay the $15 camping fee. Too bad for him, as I'm forced by Newfoundland law to buy a full six-pack of beer (single sales are not allowed) that Granny M and I can't finish despite the long, warm day. Newfoundland's own Black Horse is good beer! I leave a bottle on the table. Perhaps the bush man from Maine will sniff it out?

There's a little rain during the night to strengthen the mini rivers of condensation running off our wet tents in the morning. Granny M and I look at each other, roll our dripping garbage-bag ground sheets into a ball, and ditch them in the trash barrel. We agree that this is our last night of camping. We have long distances and just five days left to cover them in. We will pedal across this rock, but we don't have to camp. And we just don't have time for all this wet stuff.

Square Pond, Newfoundland

We are off at 6:30 a.m. under clear blue skies. Breakfast stop at Bishop's Falls takes us down and off the highway, then it's back on to the T.C.H. with more trees and lakes – could be anywhere except for the trees being scrub spruce. Large old clearcuts are not replanted. Newfoundland looks bare in spots. Fresh moose tracks on a cleared track where I stop for a pee break are at least thirty centimetres across – where is this monster? People are very friendly and unpretentious; there is no obvious evidence of wealth beyond the basics. Lunch stop is at Gander near the international airport (where 9/11 refugees from New York were hosted by Newfoundlanders for several days after the attack while New York airports were shut down). We have no time for the Aviation Museum; it pours rain during our lunch break. Later we arrrive at a small motel at Square Pond. I have partridge berry duff for dessert at dinner, a partridge berry cake with hot rum sauce and ice cream – incredibly delicious! Doing our laundry in the motel owner's laundry for free ends the day along with photographing a rainbow over Square Pond after yet another shower.

The motel owner tells me about a Literary Festival at Eastport starting the day I hope to arrive in St. John's. The roster includes famous east coast contemporary writers Lisa Moore, Alistair MacLeod, and Wayne Johnston. Would I love to go?! I find Eastport on the map and it's too far from St. John's. I don't have a chance. Maybe next time....

And there will be a next time, if at all possible. Our final few days offer a change of scene: longer hills, some with eight kilometres of up; headwinds with mostly clear skies (Newfoundland is the only province that has had a summer this year); wild blueberries just ripening on the roadside; cod's tongues for dinner; bays and inlets of the Atlantic Ocean licking the T.C.H.; pink granite rock outcroppings sheltering wee ponds and stands of wildflowers – all so representative of Newfoundland and such a phenomenal end to my odyssey. I've missed so much while getting wee glimpses and I am hooked. Newfoundland is in my blood – and my heart. I will be back!

On Wednesday, August 11, we get fifteen minutes of free email time at our motel, enough time for messages from home telling us to contact CBC radio in St. John's. Apparently our hometown media contact has connected with CBC, but how we are to connect with Canada's national radio and TV networks is vague. My husband tells me when I phone him that he has heard from his local contact person that CBC wants to film us for TV when we ride into St. John's, and gives me a Vancouver phone number. This sounds like a fantasy trying to come true. Vancouver is on the opposite side of the continent from St. John's, so not only is there a four-and-a-half hour time difference, but the likelihood of connecting with local CBC personnel via their national network seems too remote to even consider. However, my husband thinks the person I'm to contact is possibly the producer for Sheila Rogers' morning radio show. I'm a great fan of Rogers and would love to talk to her over the radio waves, so I have a flurry of excitement until cross-country phone calls once I'm in downtown St. John's prove fruitless. The answering body at CBC in Vancouver is helpful, but finally we both laugh at the charade and I give up. It was a nice thought.

On Friday, August 13, we pedal into downtown St. John's in twenty-eight degree Celsius heat over rough roads including crumbling shoulders (we've had a couple stretches of poor road conditions in spurts of heavy fog as we got closer to the city

Mile Zero, St. John's

– our final challenge!). There is road and building construction everywhere, and traffic is brisk. The highway frequently crosses exits and entrances, and I watch carefully, aware of "last day syndrome" when many accidents happen. I'm confident I won't let it happen to me. Then I have a silly minor fall when I forget to take my foot out of my toe clip when I stop – how many thousands of times have I repeated this automatic action over the last three and a half months? – and then I pitch over the handlebars when I brake suddenly to avoid a car entering the highway from my right. (Later, when I'm home, I have my brake pads replaced when I realize they are the culprit because imbedded tiny particles of grit make them grab with a jerk instead of steadily pushing against the wheel rim.) This time there are a few bruises along with roadrash and abrasions on my elbows and knees. But at the moment nothing alarming is visible or painful, and thirty minutes later we pedal up to Mile Zero of the TransCanada Highway in front of City Hall in the heart of downtown St. John's, Newfoundland on the Atlantic Ocean, 8,321 biking kilometres from Mile Zero in Victoria, B.C. on the Pacific Ocean. Today is my 105th day on the road. A passing tourist takes our photos for us. The Mile Zero banner over my head tells me I am at the beginning of Canada.

A comment in my notes of two days ago says my feelings are weird – empty! When will I wake up? And now I feel even more weird – like living inside a dream that's real. I pedal in a daze out to the suburb of Quidi Vidi, a lobster fishing village with a slipway for small boats, and dip my front wheel in the Atlantic. I'm facing east and this is the end of my journey, not the beginning as it was for all those Europeans arriving so long ago to settle the west. But even though I travelled in the opposite direction, I swayed in the wind on the prairies with the spirits of those immigrants, pulled up and over the same mountains they did, got drenched in the same rain, felt their winter chill, ate strawberries from their fields, listened to their fiddling, drank their beer and wine, almost collided with a black bear, and got driven crazy by black flies – all the while cursing and praising our wide and wonderful country. I have seen the staggering changes in landscapes, laughed and cried with people hospitable and caring beyond belief, and my admiration is as deep as all the bodies of water I have pedalled past, as wide as the skies that engulfed me, as high as the mountains I huffed and puffed up and down, and as strong as the winds that buffeted me. Thanks, Canada, for a great ride!

I'm going home for a rest!

Logistics

N ewfoundland's official title of "Newfoundland and Labrador" is such a big mouthful that few people bother to say it. However, abbreviating its name doesn't diminish either the size or the status of this easternmost province, the last to join the Confederation of Canada (in 1949). There's something that still feels new about The Rock, like the mostly refurbished TransCanada Highway connecting all the bits and pieces from the Gulf of St. Lawrence to the Atlantic coast. The highway's wide shoulders and good surface (except for brief stretches) are a treat for cyclists; 900 kilometres of trees and hills roll by quickly. There's no nonsense to the friendliness on The Rock; people are here to show you around, make you feel welcome. They really want to share their unique place with you.

Friday, August 6   (day 98).

Ride: Port-aux Basques to St. George's (B&B).
Follow T.C.H. #1. Rocky shoreline disappears into trees and more trees. Occasional gas stations on road; no other services. Carry lots of water and snacks.

Facilities: Motels, restaurants, groceries in Port-aux Basques. Camping at provincial park off highway about 20 km from ferry terminal. Next services including B&B's at St. George's; camping at Barachois Pond Provincial Park 24 km beyond St. George's.

Total distance: 137 km.
Average speed: 19 kph.
Maximum speed: 54 kph.

Saturday, August 7   (day 99).

Ride: St. George's to Steady Brook (motel).
Follow T.C.H. #1. Tough ride up and over western spine of

Newfoundland's mountains. Long stretches with no services – 70 km to lunch. Hitched a ride in rain.

Facilities: All services in Corner Brook off highway. Motels and restaurants at Steady Brook, about 10 km on highway from Corner Brook. Camping another 35 km at Deer Lake.

Total distance: 67 km plus 40 km by car.
Average speed: 16 kph.
Maximum speed: 48 kph.

Sunday, August 8 (day 100).

Ride: Steady Brook to Fort Birchey Campground.
Follow T.C.H. #1. Good road through trees, past large and small ponds; less hilly. No services on road after Deer Lake.

Facilities: Restaurant and groceries at Deer Lake. Café, laundry, snack food at campground.

Total distance: 121 km.
Average speed: 21 kph.
Maximum speed: 55 kph.

Monday, August 9 (day 101).

Ride: Fort Birchey to Grand Falls-Windsor (motel).
Follow T.C.H. #1. Long ride through no-man's land. Good road; headwinds. No services on road.

Facilities: Motels, restaurants at Grand Falls-Windsor. Camping, groceries 20 km further at Bishop's Falls.

Total distance: 138 km.
Average speed: 20 kph.
Maximum speed: 52 kph.

Tuesday, August 10 (day 102).

Ride: Grand Falls-Windsor to Square Pond (motel).
Follow T.C.H. #1. Long ride with no services for long stretches through non-replanted clearcuts.

Facilities: Motels, restaurants, T.I. in Gander. Phone ahead to reserve at small motel at Square Pond. Camping at Square Pond Park; groceries in Gander.

Total distance: 126 km.
Average speed: 19 kph.
Maximum speed: 53 kph.

Wednesday, August 11   (day 103).

Ride: Square Pond to Clarenville (motel).
Follow T.C.H. #1. Long hills through Terra Nova National Park; wild blueberries on roadside.

Facilities: Motels, restaurants, T. I. at Clarenville; email access at St. Jude's Hotel. Camping another 40 km at Arnold's Cove, groceries in Clarenville off road.

Total distance: 128 km.
Average speed: 17 kph.
Maximum speed: 55 kph.

Thursday, August 12   (day 104).

Ride: Clarenville to Moorland (motel).
Follow T.C.H. #1. No services on road. Atlantic fog a menace. Long hills, rock outcroppings, ponds.

Facilities: Motel, restaurant, T.I. at Moorland – phone to book motel as only one on road between Clarenville and St.John's; also book motel in St. John's. No camping near road between Arnold's Cove and St. John's.

Total distance: 103 km.
Average speed: 16 kph.
Maximum speed: 60 kph.

Friday, August 13   (day 105).

Ride: Moorland to St. John's Mile Zero (motel).
Follow T.C.H. #1. Follow City Centre branch of highway into downtown St. John's. Numerous exits and entrances off high-

way – watch traffic carefully! Mile Zero is in front of City Hall and Mile One Stadium on Main Street, which is continuation of highway. Dip wheels into Atlantic Ocean at Quidi Vidi's small boat slip – ask locals for directions.

Facilities: All services in St. John's. Bike shop.

Total distance: 96 km.
Average speed: 18 kph.
Maximum speed: 56 kph.

Conclusion

Our very last day on the eastern shore of Canada is spent in a bus. We are driven up Signal Hill from where Marconi made the first transatlantic wireless radio connection in the early 1900s, and then out to Cape Spear, the easternmost point on the North American continent. This is truly the end – we cannot go any further!

The next morning we are at the airport by 7:00 a.m. to bag our bikes for our flight home, knowing some people are gathering at the Calgary airport to welcome us. But I never imagined the balloons, flowers, "Welcome Home Grannies" banner – and cheers! – that greet us. What a spectacle we've made of ourselves! I'm a little embarrassed by the hoopla, and I don't brag, but I am proud of my accomplishment – and of Canada! The welcome is appreciated!

Granny M writes an email a year after we are home reminding me of our anniversary start date.

"The Cross Canada bike trip has become a highlight of my life, because up till then I hadn't really done that many road trips, so it was a huge challenge. The whole experience had an incredible impact on me, as it forced me out of several comfort zones. The adventure was one that will have me in awe for the remainder of my life. To this day I still get an excited rush whenever I reminisce about the trip."

I have moved from the town we both claimed as home a year ago, and we haven't had much contact, but our memories linger.

Lynda continues to race her triathlons, and we continue to be friends. We have no new bike adventures planned to come between us.

Paul would like to do more cycling, but hasn't managed yet. Grand Père joined me for a few days cycling the Eastern Townships in Québec in October 2005, and Sue and John and I did make it to the Magdalen Islands in September 2005. Unfortunately, that restaurant Jack Layton mentioned on the tip of the islands was closed for the season, along with most of the tourist attractions.

Strong winds thwarted our pedalling, so I still hope to return for a few days of cycling along the causeways that connect the low red hills of the French and English archipelago in the Gulf of St. Lawrence.

Phil of our Cypress Hills rescue writes in September 2004:

"I am now back in Prince Albert, Saskatchewan ... at SIAST teaching within the Natural Resource Technology Department..... Rest assured that "La Vielle Citrouille is still alive and well. Prior to my journey North, I installed a new clutch, replaced the old radiator and front brake caliper. I am now well prepared to transport bricks, hay, fence posts and other miscellaneous items back and forth to the acreage (as well as being able to transport eclectic cyclists in distress if need be)......I had a wonderful time assisting you folks across the Cypress Hills into the Frenchman Valley of Eastend.....I had an inspiring moment at Jone's Peak and look forward to the pictures.....I would like to take this opportunity to congratulate each of you for you accomplishments.....And thank you for allowing me to play a small and brief role in your adventure....(I am now inspired to become as adventuresome in my senior years as you all have demonstrated).....Philippe."

Gloria and Ken, our storm rescuers in Saskatchewan, write a Bravo! email and remind us that we are an inspiration to them all:

"And hopefully you will enjoy some well deserved rest, although we will miss your updates!"

More bravos have arrived from Canadians met along the way, plus friends from around the world – I've hooked more than I realized with my updates and Canadian adventures. Audiences at my slide shows tell me I'm an inspiration – to cyclists, to women, and to seniors. My biggest wish is that I will encourage more Canadians to explore their own country, preferably on their bikes!

What did I learn from my bike ride with a twist? The answer could stretch to infinity – but most significantly, I learned to believe in myself, to pursue my ideals, to care for my body as well as my spirit, to carry food at all times, to forget about cooking en route (as well as high-tech gadgets), and keep on pedalling.

I also learned that designated campsites are almost always too noisy and too expensive, but are preferred over free-camping in the bush without facilities.

I found that most people whom I encountered while on my bike were curious and considerate and treated me with respect. In turn, I learned to respect Canada – its vast areas of land and its differences in people who, ultimately, aren't very different after all. Different languages, different cultures, and different food and music and art do not obscure our bottom line. We are all Canadians who are free to choose, and bound by our choices.

P.S. I have not had another broken spoke – not even one!

What I took with me

Trek 520 touring bike
    drop handlebars with gear and brake cables
    cantilever brakes
    triple crankset with 1:1 gear ratio, 52 on front chain ring
    Panaracer Tourer Tires, folding, size 700 x 35, one spare
    two spare tubes

Tools: flat repair kit with tire irons, multi-tool with Allen keys and screw drivers, small pliers, pedal wrench, spoke tool and extra spokes cut to fit front and rear wheels, chain tool, foot pump

Lights: rear blinking, front triple beam halogen head light/flash light

Extra nuts, bolts, screws

Small winding of duct tape and masking tape, wire twist ties

Lubricant and chain-cleaning rag

Heavy cable lock

Helmet

Bollé sport sun glasses with prescription lens insert

Sleeping bag, Therm-a-Rest sleeping pad and folding chair, sleep-sheet liner for sleeping bag, inflatable pillow

Tarp and nylon line

Eureka single person tent

MSR Pocketrocket camp stove with two canisters fuel, matches, one aluminum cooking pot, plastic utensils and dishes, salt & pepper and dried herbs, plastic bottle for oil, ziplock bags, biodegradable camping soap, Swiss army knife, dishcloth/towel, pot-scrubber

Two water bottles plus hydration backpack

Sheepskin saddle cover

Two front and two rear panniers with waterproof plastic liners; small removable handlebar bag for camera, money (a few traveller's cheques for rural areas and no bank), picture ID, address book (with email addresses), bike ID card, provincial medical insurance card, notebook

Map holder for handlebar, waterproof

Camera, film, maps, books, notebooks, pens, pencil, highlighter

First aid kit, medications, vitamin supplements

Personal items: camping towel, swim suit, toiletries (travel miniatures), alarm clock, two cycling shorts and short sleeve tops, one long-sleeve jersey and tights for the mountains, shorts and teeshirt for warmer weather off bike, one long pants and shirt for dress, bike shoes and socks, Teva sandals, fleece jacket, rain jacket (layered with fleece jacket in cold temperatures) and rain pants and helmet cover and booties, extra warm gloves in mountains, cycling gloves, wind-breaker cycling jacket and vest, sun hat with bug screen, small scarf/bandanna, one extra bra and underpants, laundry kit, sun screen, bug spray, tissues, prescription glasses

A hint about packing: roll clothing and pack in plastic bags according to use – shirts in one bag, shorts in another, socks and underwear in another, etc. Rule of thumb is one outfit on, one clean outfit packed. Keep rain gear together and easily accessible. Make sure all books and maps are in waterproof ziplock bags.

What I spent

Budget:
On a daily basis, I spent on average $60 per day when I motelled and ate in restaurants. When I camped and picnicked, I spent on average $30 per day. This was for basic accommodation and food.

Bike maintenance costs included routine cleaning and tuneups whenever I encountered a bike shop. I did not attempt to maintain my bike on my own. And then there were always extras for repairs and replacement parts. This can be a large budget item on a long bike ride, and three and a half months pedalling across Canada was no exception. One needs to budget accordingly.

Other expenses:
Transportation to and from starting points. My WestJet airplane ticket St. John's to Calgary was $420 plus an extra $60 for bike transport. I was driven by car to Victoria, B.C. to begin the trip.

Clothing and gear replaced along the way along with tourist attraction costs were extras as were communication (emails and telephone) expenses.

Preparing for the trip included some additional camping gear as well as upgrades to my bike.

Bibliography

Butala, Sharon. *Lilac Moon*. Toronto: HarperCollins Publishers Ltd, 2005.

——— . *Old Man on his Back*. Toronto: HarperCollins Publishers Ltd, 2002.

——— . *The Perfection of the Morning*. Toronto: HarperCollins Publishers Ltd, 1994.

Faragher, John Mack. *A Great and Noble Scheme: the Expulsion of the French Acadians*. New York & London: W. W. Norton, 2005.

Fiennes, William. *The Snow Geese*. New York: Random House, 2002.

Hill, Charles C.. *Group of Seven.* Toronto: McClelland & Stewart, 1995.

Langford, Dan & Sandra. *Cycling the Kettle Valley Railway*. Calgary: Rocky Mountain Books, 1994, 3rd edition, 2002.

Longfellow, William Wadsworth. *Poems and other Writings*. Toronto: Penguin Group (Canada), 2000.

Mussio, Russell & Marleau, Jason. *Trans Canada Trail the British Columbia Route*. New Westminster, B.C.: Mussio Ventures Ltd, 2001.

Mustoe, Anne. *A Bike Ride*. London: Virgin Books, 1991. www.annemustoe. co.uk/books

Stegner, Wallace. *Wolf Willow*. New York: Viking Press, 1955, 1957, 1958, 1959, 1962.

Wood, Daniel & Sinclair, Beverley. *Western Journeys.* Vancouver: Raincoast Books, 1997.